Mercury

The Winged Messenger

By

Courtney L. Zietzke

First published by Author House 04/15/04

ISBN: 1-4140-2644-7 (e-book)
ISBN: 1-4184-3781-6 (Paperback)

This book is printed on acid free paper.

FOREWARD

"What the hell is going on?!", I said quietly to my office nurse as I walked out of the exam room, leaving behind another distraught family with a child diagnosed with Autism. They had come to my office for help after being told by other physicians there was nothing that could be done. Since no tests were done to determine the **cause** of their child's sudden neurological regression, no treatment was given because there was no apparent cure.

My heart was broken by the tragedy these families were experiencing. I'm the eldest of five children and have a daughter of my own. I know the joy of a healthy child and the devastation that the diagnosis of illness, especially of a neurological impairment such as Autism. Before medical school, I had attained a Master's degree in Biology, specializing in Genetics and Microbiology. I had also worked as a scientist in vaccine research and development. This background provided the basis for me to be intrigued about this tragic medical phenomenon I was seeing in my office.

I had become educated in the effects of various environmental neurotoxins in my patients. These patients had been labeled with a variety of diagnoses that related to their neurotoxic **symptoms**, such as Attention Deficit Disorder, Obsessive Compulsive Disorder, Depression, Multiple Sclerosis, Chronic Fatigue and Fibromyalgia, The actual biochemical **causes** had not been evaluated. It was during my graduate school education prior to medical school that I studied abnormal biochemical and hormonal pathways.

I was taught in medical school and residency to identify symptoms, make a diagnosis and prescribe a pharmaceutical drug or recommend surgery. I was not trained to determine the abnormal biochemical pathway. I raised my hand often and didn't hesitate to question the faculty. At the end of my first year of medical school, I was voted by my classmates as "Most Likely to Quit Medical School and Become an Attorney". I took it as a compliment, I'm still not sure it was meant as one.

I was shocked by the epidemic number of children being diagnosed with Autism in the U.S. during recent years. The numbers were real, not a matter of over-labeling or a less stringent criteria being employed. The numbers come from the U.S. Department of Education as required by the Individuals With Disabilities Education Act of 1975. This legislation requires that disabled children be provided "free appropriate public education." Initially, autistic children in school were so rare that the category was lumped with other disabilities. Exponential increases in the number (5,415) of autistic children resulted in Autism be listed as a separate entity in 1991. The number of autistic children reported in 2001 had risen to a stunning 118,600 known cases! Remember this is a report from the U.S. Department of Education **not** the Department of Health, nor the Centers for Disease Control.

I began to investigate this situation by talking to parents of Autistic children and researching the literature. I was struck by the common description of perfectly normal children suddenly regressing at eighteen months, losing their speech, interactive personalities and suddenly becoming hypersensitive to stimuli, noises and changes in their environment. Parents described these events as happening a few months after the last multiple vaccine series had been administered to their children.

The Zietzke family told me a similar story. I remember when Ian's parents, Courtney and Venus showed me the Pediatrician's hand written descriptors on Ian's medical record of "Great Shape" at the 2 week and 2 month well child visits. The comment written by the Pediatrician on the 4 month examination record by the Pediatrician was "Beautiful Specimen", at the 9 month visit "Fantastic" was written. What happened to Ian between the diagnosis of "Beautiful Specimen" and Autism at age 2? Ian's toxic environmental exposure included from age 2 months to 15 months a total of thirteen Thimerosal-containing vaccines. A total of five live vaccines containing attenuated Measles and Polio viruses were also administered to Ian from 2 months to 15 months of age.

The epidemic numbers reminded me of the Thalidomide tragedy of the early 1960's. Thousands of children in Great Britain and Europe were born with out arms or legs, mimicking a genetic defect called Amelia (born without arms or legs) or Phycomelia (born with shortened arms and legs). It took several years for the significant increase in these birth defects to be recognized as due to the ingestion of the drug Thalidomide for the treatment of nausea by thousands of women in the first trimester of pregnancy.

I wondered if there were a similar situation causing an epidemic of children with Autism in the USA. As I read the research related to the study of Autistic children, it became clear to me, that the major change that had occurred in the past twenty years was related to toxicity issues, especially the addition of Thimerosal, a mercury derivative that was used as a preservative in many infant vaccines. The preservative Thimerosal was banned in dog vaccines and optometric solutions many years ago due to safety issues. Finally in 2003, Thimerosal was banned in infant vaccines. Thimerosal is still used as a preservative in Influenza vaccine.

Questions nagged at my mind, just as they had other researchers and parents. Why were there so many cases in the U.S. in recent years? Had these parents done anything to cause this? What was the link to Thimerosal-containing vaccines? Did the use of attenuated measles vaccine or the number of vaccines given to an infant contribute to an immune reaction leading to a breakdown of the blood brain barrier or a breach of the integrity of the gut leading to immune dysfunction?. Why did the Federal Government and Pediatricians abdicate responsibility to their families by steadfastly promoting vaccines with the known neurotoxin Thiomersal? Why were parents told they were "bad and irresponsible" if they refused vaccines for their children? Why have studies carefully researching the effect of heavy metals and other neurotoxins not been done in this country?. Why do we have to rely on Canada, Great Britain and European studies for the truth? And finally, what did the federal government know and when did they know it? Why did the Homeland Security Bill have a middle-of-the-night amendment added to it which prevents the children and their families from suing the responsible parties in this scandalous tragedy?

The positive side to this story is that the word is out. Thimerosal has been banned in infant vaccines. The diagnosis of heavy metal toxicity is easy, safe, inexpensive and accurate. All that is required in children is an injection of DMPS, followed by a nine hour urine collection. The lab can analyze the urine sample for toxic heavy metals. If urine cannot be collected due to incontinence, DMPS can be give orally. A stool sample is collected 48 hours later and sent to the lab for analysis. Based upon these results appropriate diagnosis and treatment protocols can be instituted. In my office we have seen spectacular results with heavy metal detoxification in autistic children. I have several children who were severe in their symptoms, i.e. non-verbal, non-communicative, who after just three or four treatments with DMPS regain speech. One six year now counts loudly and clearly to 25 as he receives his injection.

The information presented in this book is informed, compelling, thought provoking and emotionally charged. Capitalism goes wrong when we can deliberately, with knowledge and fore-thought, poison our infants in the chase of the almighty dollar. It is the countries with socialized medicine, where governments find it in their own best interest, to determine the truth and correct the problem.

When we as a society, in the richest, most advanced country in the world, decide to take responsibility for our actions, corporate greed and political corruption will no longer rule the land.

Submitted by:

Lyn Hanshew, M.D.
Bellevue, WA U.S.A.

This book is dedicated to Ian N. Zietzke, A delicate and beautiful soul......................

It was the summer of 1987; the Republican agenda was in full swing and was beginning to pick a new successor to President, Ronald Reagan. It was obvious to many that our next President would be the Vice President, George H. W. Bush.

In these years, the political establishment was building an immense financial and political power base that would undermine the publics trust for years to come.

The pawns and ultimate victims in this money grab would be the most innocent of all people…..

Our children.

Table Of Contents

INTRODUCTION

As a parent of an Autistic child, it is difficult to describe the pain and resentment that is felt by having a perfect baby and then having that baby snatched from you at about 16 months old.

The brain damage that my child received should not have happened. The U.S. healthcare industry is the best in the World. There are safeguards and redundancies built into the system. However, in this case, the system failed and failed badly.

My child and countless others were injected with a substance known as Thimerosal.

Thimerosal is an additive to baby vaccines that contains 49.6% Mercury. This substance was banned by the pet vaccination industry over ten years ago because of known health risks. The pharmaceutical industry kept this additive in the baby vaccines, knowing full well the risks to our children's health.

According to my child's weight and the amount of vaccines he received that contained this additive, my child and thousands of other children have received over 40 times the legal safety limit for mercury exposure as established by the Environmental Protection Agency.

I speak for literarily thousands of concerned and angry parents who basically got burned by a system that has been perverted by Greed, Politics, and Corruption.

In the last several years, the Food and Drug Administration (FDA), the Centers of Disease Control (CDC) and the National Institutes of Health (NIH) have granted hundreds of waivers of the conflict of interest rule in favor of the drug giants and their "paid consultants". Has the U.S. health care system been unduly influenced? Thousands of children have suffered the consequences of these people's greed and short sightedness.

My child was born perfectly healthy, full of life. He had the potential to achieve anything in life that he would have chosen to do.

Because of a short sighted medical system that failed, my child is now a semi vegetative little boy who is lost in his own tortured world of mercury induced autism.

This book talks about the cause and the arrogant atmosphere that abounds in the vaccine community that has caused this tragedy.

If you look at an autistic child, you will notice fear and profound sadness on their little faces. They are imprisoned in a world where they desperately want to escape, but can't.

The frustration that these children feel and their cries for help have been ignored by the very system that caused this atrocity.

When I look upon other healthy six year old children who are playing, communicating and living normal lives, I wonder what might have been with my little boy. I am sure I am not alone in my thoughts. This is a painful and very tragic occurrence.

Instead of concern, sympathy and needed help, the Pharmaceutical industry and the "system" that caused this tragedy has been for the most part unsympathetic, evasive and full of legal denials.

This book will anger many people, which is precisely what it is intended to do.

My desire is to light a fire under the bureaucrats, politicians and the medical community to get off their asses and do something to help these children. These children did not deserve what they got.

The parents of these brain damaged children have suffered terrible pain and financial hardship as a result of the greed and political corruption from the very segment of our society that was supposed to invoke trust and medical excellence.

Is this book critical? You bet it is. I know I speak for thousands of people who, like myself want answers. The tragic truth is that every time a question is asked, all that is given in return is deception, distorted truths and out right lies from the very people we trusted the most.

Lastly, it is my hope that this book will at least get people asking the questions of HOW?, WHO? And most importantly, WHY DID THIS HAPPEN TO THOUSANDS OF INNOCENT CHILDREN?

During the mid 1980's and early 1990's the Center for Disease Control (CDC) and many other U.S. governmental health departments were continuing to work with and in conjunction with the pharmaceutical industry toward thwarting diseases from our society. The monetary rewards for doing this were immense. It is well known that the U.S. pharmaceutical industry is a multi billion dollar, multi national conglomerate, mega industry. These people today are politically powerful and they are very, very rich.

Seeing that this immense opportunity existed, the executive and legislative branches of our government along with the pharmaceutical industry went to work about designing a vaccine program that would gain the public awareness as a good and just program for all concerned and put one hell of a lot of money in the pockets of the pharmaceutical industry and the GOP.

The public relations machine in the pharmaceutical industry and the federal government went to work in designing a public workshop type of environment that created a trust relationship between the pharmaceutical companies, the federal government and the general public. As a result, the CDC, FDA, NIH and the Department of Health issued new and comprehensive guidelines in recommending children's health vaccines. Children are the largest segment in our society that receives routine vaccinations.

The scope of this new policy was sweeping. This new approach was warmly accepted as a public good. Later, the Department of Education was systematically brought on board and eventually mandated the policies adopted as "the new vaccine policy".

For many years, many prominent physicians, scientists and health care professionals who started out working in public health, had also climbed the ranks to hold senior positions in the Pharmaceutical industry. Many of these people held patents or had financial interests in many of the vaccines and patented delivery systems that were now being recommended for children's vaccine protocols.

The Pharmaceutical industry was poised to make literally tens of billions of dollars because of this new and accepted public policy in protecting our children from diseases. The politicians successfully incorporated all necessary governmental agencies to work in cooperation with these new mandates.

The sky was the limit. The pharmaceutical industry's sales exploded and of course, the politicians received "donations" and the usual "gifts". This was a lobbyist's dream come true. Major new policies were being initiated at the state and federal levels concerning children's vaccine protocols.

The results of these efforts had created layer upon layer of bureaucracy surrounding the health care industry, this especially true concerning children's vaccines.

The environment that was created in the public's perception was a warm, friendly and caring environment that was carried by posters and information circulars to literally every children's clinic across this country. The vaccines were a matter of public good and were necessary for children of all ages. In fact, these vaccines were now mandatory if a child wanted to attend public schools. The Department of Health Education and Welfare made damn sure of it. (The New Vaccine Policy)

By making vaccines mandatory for all school children, the federal government basically guaranteed the Pharmaceutical industry's profits for years to come.

Does the federal government require a person to buy an automobile? Does the U.S Government require a person to buy a certain brand of bread? Vaccinations were at one time by choice. After these policies were initiated, there was no choice.

When children are born today, they are required to have a Hepatitis B vaccination right out of the womb. Hepatitis B, at that age? Was this undue influence by the drug industry? A hepatitis B vaccine is not cheap. Later, it was determined that this vaccination was totally unnecessary. It was also determined that this vaccine was loaded with something very harmful to all children. The vaccine industry made millions on that one policy. Policies surrounding children's vaccine protocols are all geared to benefit the drug industry. This was by design and it will become very apparent in this book as to why this is the case.

The federal agencies were compliant with these children's vaccine protocols, the Republican / GOP were getting huge political donations and the pharmaceutical company's were getting rich beyond their wildest imagination. Their stocks across the board jumped and exploded in value.

Many governmental people and policy makers at the federal and state levels who held pharmaceutical stocks watched their stock portfolios increase many times…..They got rich.

Many of the physicians who worked in the governmental health agencies also held lucrative stock positions in this industry. It is a documented fact that these people also had special royalty arrangements with the pharmaceutical companies. They also got rich.

The executive and legislative branches of the United States Government in conjunction with the pharmaceutical industry who had proposed and had initiated this vaccine policy were "pleased" with the results of this sweeping policy, all done for the public good. Everybody was a winner………… Except many our children.

Their damaged lives and their parents' worse nightmare was still to come…..

When George H.W. Bush was nominated for the presidency of the United States, he needed a Vice President that could help him in three ways.

1. Low profile; a man who would never challenge his political agendas while in office.
2. A moderate republican who is from our heartland who would be perceived as a young and dynamic person who would accept the role as Vice President as the greatest honor ever bestowed on a young senator.
3. Well connected politically, intelligent and very well connected in business.

In the 1988 presidential campaign George Bush introduced Senator Dan Quayle (R. Indiana) this was a marriage made in heaven. Quayle was a young senator who was connected with big business and who fit the mold in what George Bush needed.

This marriage was also good in other ways that was as subtle and undetectable as one could ever imagine.

History proved once again that a strong Republican President is followed into office by another Republican. George Bush easily captured the presidency. Ronald Reagan successfully rewarded his Vice President with new home, The White House. Ronald Reagan faded into the history books.

With a new government and with health care mandates already in full swing, all was in place to literally make billions of dollars in an industry where no one ever asked questions. Why should they? It's the government; with the all knowing physicians and staff people who know that there way was the best way. If anyone ever challenged their policies, they were either fired out right or were embarrassed by five other people who had the credentials to bury any criticism. Any questions were immediately referred to a committee where it was buried by protocols and piles of paper bureaucracy.

Government physicians, researchers and politicians who had helped mandate the vaccine policy and who held stock, continued to make literally millions and millions of dollars.

Stocks and personal wealth exploded in the drug industry and all was fantastic. The GOP was receiving huge political donations and the vice president was performing as a vice president should. He never publicly questioned the President on any agenda.

This was interesting, because the Vice Presidents job is to keep the President on his toes. Remember, if the President is unable to perform the duties as President, then the Vice President assumes the duties immediately. The Vice President was very quiet during this time period. Was something wrong?

During the vice presidential selection process, Bush had already known the advantages in selecting Quayle, he was young, connected and of course the Quayle family controlled much of the drug giant, Eli Lilly & Co. of Indiana.

These people had huge money and were very powerful political donors to the Republican presidential campaign. This is still the case in today's world.

In fact, Bush sat on the board of directors of Lilly Co. for a number of years. This was the manifest destiny, a predetermined union and was the payback to the Quayle (Lilly) family for Bush's previous appointment to the board of directors of Eli Lilly Co. This is a documented fact.

The people who put Bush into office were very rich and powerful people. As a result, The White House agenda was oil, defense industries and of course the pharmaceutical industry. The White House accommodated these special interest groups to a tee.

The U.S. commitment in the gulf war was manufactured by Special Interests and their political "alliances" in order to get the government to justify and to pay for war items that would enhance the profits of these three industries. This was done under the guise of National Security. When President Eisenhower left office, he warned the American people years ago to watch out for these powerful, special interest groups.

National Security was and still is a favorite of politicians who for some unknown reason cannot say they are screwing the public over with their lies and deceptions about a useless agenda, "perceived threat" or program that is only designed to profit the rich, powerful industrialists who, along with their political friends are milking the system for their own advantage, all at the expense of the American taxpayer.

During this Gulf war, who made money? ... Who? ...What did the U.S. actually gain? Access to oil? Stability? Recent world events clearly show that the Administration at that time had made major foreign policy mistakes that has resulted in the world today that is very unstable and much more dangerous. Many innocent people have died as a result of the Gulf war.

During the Gulf war, the pharmaceutical industry was a huge winner. Pharmaceutical stocks & options sky rocketed in value. Vaccines were given out in record numbers and were pushed into heavy production because of NATIONAL SECURITY!

The main stream media swallowed this hole and reported all facets of the war in their usual pro government/corporate slant. The media was and still is a public relations tool for the rich. They will wag their tales to get a treat and bark at those who piss them off by using "bad press" to discredit an opponent. Freedom of press?..... Freedom of speech?...... sounds good?......sounds fair?........It ISN'T!

The press can and does destroy people and opponents of powerful corporate interests. These powerful interests either use bad press against their opponents or simply fail to report the whole truth that would even the score, even when these powerful interests are clearly in the wrong.

The corporations control the press and the press controls public opinion, this is because they both control a lot of money and money talks over all else. There have been many sides to many stories that never get full press coverage. Is the main stream press being enhanced by U.S. policy? Absolutely! The owners of mainstream newspapers and magazines are powerful people who can obviously mandate and manipulate public opinion through the pages of their news papers and their magazine empires.

Sensationalizing stories for the benefit of corporate advertising powers (who are the powerful governmental "favorites") will sell newspapers. Many powerful multi national corporations own news papers and major media markets. It is also a fact that corporations like General Electric own radio and TV networks. In the last twenty years media consolidation and corporate controlled media has become a reality in America. These people control press coverage for their own benefit.

During the time of the early 90's President Bush vetoed the minimum wage bill. Also, during the Bush years, the president went along with and voted with congress to give itself a 35 % pay raise at 2:00 am in the early morning hours. I guess the government didn't need sleep that night.

The only real in depth press coverage was by the Grace Commission. It was hardly mentioned in any of the major publications. When the President vetoed the minimum wage and then gave his colleagues in congress the big pay increase, this should have said to the people who knew that there was a big problem. The press only reported small details of this. Why is this fact important to this book? It sets the general tone of greed and feudalism of the powerful, pro governmental / corporate interest framework, that controls the public relations machine for key industry's, namely the industrial military complex, oil and of course the drug giants.

This should have been a huge story. Millions of people didn't get the help they needed to make a living. Why didn't the press give this more coverage? Why didn't the press sensationalize this like they do so often for stories that would benefit the rich and powerful? The powers that were at that time and the President didn't give a damn about the working poor or the middle class people in this country, they never did then and they never have since.

Not all press is bias; there are many smaller publications that are dedicated to the **truth**. Unfortunately, these enterprises lack funding to become main stream.

The **truth** is what this books talks about. The subject in this book needs more in depth exposure and honest reporting. The truth has come out and the main stream press is only beginning to discuss what has happened in a limited way. My point is that the truth should have been reported on much earlier, because if it would have, thousands of children would have been saved. On time reporting and transparency would have made a big difference. This national tragedy could have been avoided.

People say that the main stream press is too liberal. I disagree. The press is only liberal on selected subjects that will sell newspapers. They want people to think they are liberal so they won't be accused of being too biased. The main stream media giants will protect their own and have done so on many occasions.

If I were the richest man in the world, could I get my story published?

If I was a child who was not able to talk, would somebody listen to my tragedy?

If this tragedy was caused by the political, powerful, rich and connected people would it ever be reported on by a somewhat bias press? That is why this work is in print.

My name is Ian N. Zietzke, I am 6 years old. I was born to a happy family in Seattle, WA on December 10, 1996

During my gestation period, I was a perfectly healthy baby boy who showed no signs of being developmentally disabled.

After my birth, the doctors told my parents that I was a perfect little boy.

I hit all baby milestones. In fact, I exceeded many of them. I have film and pictures that show me as a happy and very healthy baby boy with no brain damage what so ever.

During the first 16 months of my life, my parents were told by the doctor that I had to have my baby vaccines. They were told that they must comply or I would not be admitted to school. My mom and dad did what the doctors had said because it was in my best interest and it would prevent disease. Mom and dad trusted these vaccines.

The shots hurt me and I cried. All I could do was to try to tell mommy that something was starting to happen to me. I was loosing my focus and I started to feel intense pain.

I tried to talk but I was loosing my ability to even to try to talk. My ears were ringing all of the time and I was never hungry anymore. I cried and was really afraid. I was really sensitive to light. I would walk on my tip toes because I was starting to loose my senses.

Courtney L. Zietzke

As I received more vaccines, I really started to hurt. My brain was numbing and I was crying more and more. Finely, I lost all speech and all understanding of my environment.

My parents are devastated. My mommy and daddy cry because I cannot talk or function.

I have been given tests and I was diagnosed with "Autism". This is a life time label that will never go away. My life now is filled with strange images and distorted sights.

I cry everyday and I feel intense fear and pain. I am afraid and I cannot go to the bathroom. My brain is sick and I need help.

This is the life of my little boy Ian. He and countless others were the ultimate victims of the worst greed in human history, carried out by the very people we trusted most.

During the early 90's the presidential campaign turned to the economy.

President Bush was soundly defeated by Bill Clinton.

During the Clinton years, the economy improved and people got back to work.

Also, during the Clinton Years, The pharmaceutical industry made more and more money. A lot more money. The people who had previously mandated the vaccine programs were getting richer as well….A lot richer.

No one noticed a potential problem and why not, everything was great!

Back in the mid 90's the vaccine program was in full swing. The vaccine producers were making and selling huge quantities of vaccines all for the public good. They obviously wanted more and more shareholder value. Why not? Everyone is pleased and every one of the shareholders deserves to be richer.

Why not continue to package the vaccines in multiple dose containers? The pharmaceutical company's will be able to minimize the costs even further and make even more money.

While all of this was going on, a few people began to question the wisdom of vaccinating these children with so many vaccines. Was this really necessary?

Many health care professionals were beginning to worry about possible side affects and were beginning to ask…But wait, will this be safe…..? Will I get sued if something goes wrong ….? Well, they already added an agent that will preserve the integrity of the vaccine. So, we will be ok. This agent is an odorless, white powder that is a sterilizing agent that will insure purity. Great, we are covered.

The pharmaceutical company's sold more and more vaccines and minimized their costs. The political - Pharmaceutical side which had mandated these vaccine policies was stable and were largely unchecked, and why not!

During the years of 1993 -1999 something happened. Children were beginning to slip away. Parents were noticing that their children were exhibiting neurological damage.

As a result, many parents started to ask questions. "What's happening"?

How can this be? They received all of their vaccines. All of the policy makers and the drug companies who are looking out for these children could not understand. "Oh my god", can it be Autism? ………. "We are so sorry about your child".

At the present time, the autism epidemic has exploded in the U.S and the U.K.

Through the years of the Clinton Administration all health concerns were directed to the federal agencies which previously mandated all of the requirements to vaccinate children. They knew something was wrong...."we are so sorry". Committees were formed and a few enlightened souls were even concerned about the possibly of Mercury in the vaccines, that may have accumulated and caused damage to many of these children.

The pharmaceutical industry was taken aback by this insulting and rude line of questioning. How dare these concerned people question our science and integrity!

We are the powerful drug industry. We know what's best. Committees and more committees. Then finely, in 1999, they removed **Thimerosal** from the vaccines.

WHY? They said it was safe! Now they suddenly change their minds? Could it be Mercury poisoning?

The pharmaceutical industry did this only a precaution and to placate the concerned few. Well ok, now where are we? They will remove the mercury. Great! Did they remove the mercury from all of the vaccines including the vaccines that were still on the shelves? Of course not, that would cost the industry millions of dollars. It would also begin to arouse public suspicion, that maybe; just maybe, we had a problem.

The drug giants like many multi national corporations, have long range strategic planning committees. These people are paid to think about the future, plan for the worst and take steps to ensure the company will be profitable and never loose shareholder value.

The financial community refers to this as owner wealth maximization. This owner wealth theory carries over to all aspects of the corporate tree and all facets of the company and its divisions, both domestic and international.

Many years ago, the drug industry along with their think tanks realized that business was going to get good. They employed their strategic planners and came up with a solution to a future problem. Remember, these people have the politicians in their pockets, with their political power and under the guise of national security, a winning combination.

Congress passed the (NVIP) National Vaccine Injury Program in 1986.

This act essentially provides a three year statute of limitations on which to file a claim against the pharmaceutical industry for injuries sustained in vaccine injury cases.

Congress claims this act was supposed to speed up injury claims to the injured.

In actuality, it does the exact opposite. Here is why….

If a person is harmed from a vaccine and if they choose to file a claim, they must go through a vaccine court. This person must hire a lawyer, go through the discovery process then obviously file the claim.

The pharmaceutical industry will have their lawyers as well as the governmental lawyers defending the case in this court. This is already an unfair battle. This vaccine court is in a Federal jurisdiction. The government has unlimited funds in which to defend this litigation. The pharmaceutical industry has more money then most countries. Both sets of defense lawyers have been vigorously defending all suits of this type. They know that if they were to loose even a minor a case, it could set a precedent. These people will use all means at their disposal to either win a case or have it dismissed outright. So far, they have won or dismissed almost every case.

The plaintiff has for the most part already lost their case even before they file a claim.

The plaintiff is essentially going to court against two defendants. The Government and the drug giants and it's in a Federal Government court!.....Good luck!

The statute of limitations is three years in which to file a claim in vaccine court. In all cases of criminal law and most civil law cases, the statute of limitations has been and shall always be for seven years. Again, the powerful have squashed the innocent, and this time they got the government to do it for them and in their own vaccine court.

Why did the pharmaceutical industry strategically plan that they may need this kind of protection? They knew back before 1986 that there was going to be big problems.

They got their governmental "partners" through the legislative process to enact a law and even incept a new Court of "law" that gave them a blue sky future with no possibility of any liability. Did they know something before hand?

During the later half of the Clinton years, more and more children were being vaccinated and at earlier times in their lives. The pharmaceutical industry said it was for protection and it was for the good of all other children.

Because the pharmaceutical industry had developed the multi dose bottles in which to administer the injections, the profitability per injection was increased because the costs in the packaging was substantially decreased. Therefore, the cost per injection was much lower. Being mindful of the owner wealth maximization / shareholder value mind set, the pharmaceutical representatives or reps went to tens of thousands of medical clinics across the country in order to show the baby vaccine products and to buy the physician the usual free lunch and give out the customary free pens and medical goodies. This was to reassure physicians that all was "ok" and to speed up the vaccine schedule in infants.

In the early to mid 90's the medical clinics responded to governmental guidelines and began to inject infants with three and four vaccines per visit. After all, this was for the good of the people and of course it's a government mandated program....Our friends in the Governmental health community! "In God We Trust".

The immunization posters emulating children playing in a park with flowers and a happy family that was disease free was a powerful message that everybody bought.

However, within this happy sphere was the deadly reality that these vaccines contained the chemical called THIMEROSAL. This was the white powder that was the sterilization mechanism that enabled the drug companies to cut their costs and maximize their profits from multi dose bottles. Thimerosal is 49.6% MERCURY!

Not only did this industry cut their costs by enabling multi injection bottles to be on the market which contained this thimerosal, they also encouraged that the injections be given simultaneously three and four at a time, thereby making money faster and faster. They could not get this product into these children fast enough......Share holder value!

While all these millions of infants were being injected with the vaccines at the rate of three and four injections per visit, a trend began to develop.......Autism.

Autism is a neurological disorder that happens in early childhood. All speech is lost or fails to develop. The child slips into a semi vegetative state, has no focus, does not eat and has strange behavior characteristics.

Autism is a wide spectrum disorder that is very difficult to describe and quantify.
It is especially difficult to treat. Nobody really knows what the hell it is.

The pharmaceutical industry has consistently denied that their products caused Autism in thousands of children. Yet the rate of autism has increased over 700% in the last 10 years. This rate of occurrence is directly related to when our friends, the rich and powerful increased the frequency and dosages of the multi dose baby vaccines that were given to our children. These vaccines contained the thimerosal.

Since Autism is a spectrum disorder, no one can tell how bad a child has this disorder and sadly, a child who cannot talk is obviously not much good at telling his parents what's wrong.

The sad truth about this whole autism diagnoses is that when the parents finely pin down the truth what may have been their child's condition, the legal statute of limitations would have ran out. Remember the three year statute rule in the governmental / pharmaceutical court? The court where you don't have a chance in hell! At present many legal suits have been dismissed because the Statute of Limitations has already run out on which to file a case. Well, I guess that pretty much finishes this subject. The parents and their children loose, game over. The three year statute has already expired in the vaccine court.........SORRY!

The parents who can prove that their child was injured by the vaccines will not get a fair hearing because the vaccine court is controlled by the pharmaceutical industry and the current law says that all vaccine claims must go through this court. .....Do we have a chance? Can we prove injury? Will we get a fair trial?

YES is the answer to these questions. These innocent victims and their parents can win.......Here is how.

On Jan 4th 2001, The United States swore in a new president.... another Bush.

This Bush is like his father........ and.......... not like his father. This man is intelligent, he is savvy and is a loyal republican, almost to a fault and that fault will be the pharmaceutical company's and the governments Achilles tendon.

The pharmaceutical company's being bothered by the facts presented by numerous colleagues that their vaccine products may be causing damage moved quickly to reaffirm their political clout among the politicians. These in particular were the Republicans who have enjoyed the vast donations and prosperity over the last decade.

On the legal front, they were moving quietly in the judicial system to reaffirm their clout in maintaining the vaccine injury court that they had established years earlier with the federal government as their personal guardian and watch dog.

Watch Dog, a canine pet ...Here is a FACT.......... The pet industry took Thimerosal out of pet vaccines over ten years ago because of the risks of mercury poisoning to animals. The pharmaceutical industry knew the dangers.

The Government of the United States of America also knew what was going to happen to these children over ten years ago.

In fact, the U.S. government knew that Lilly Pharmaceutical Company intentionally distorted information and failed to report the facts on Thimerosal as early as 1929. The U.S. Government did absolutely nothing to protect these innocent children from harm.

They instead enacted a law that simply protects their rich, powerful pharmaceutical friends in their company owned courts of law, the vaccine courts. They weighed the possible loss of children against the profits of the industry and made their choice. The results and the brain damage to children years later are horrifying.

A media vice president of a well known drug giant issued a statement to the press saying that "These law suits that claim that our products cause autism have no bases in reality"!

Reality: A condition of fact: A child is partially brain damaged because of multiple mercury Injections over a years period. A child has no blood brain barrier nor does a child have a developed immune system that would eliminate this poison from their systems. The target organs in mercury poisoning are Brain, Spleen, Bone and the central nervous system….. Reality? Yes, a very painful one!

The informed internet parents of the new millennium have figured out what may have happened to their children. A lot of very bright people and a few honest physicians have put together a vast amount of data that supports what the government's Institute of Medicine (I.O.M.) calls a "plausible" theory. Plausible?……Are they kidding?

When you inject a baby with what amounts to as 40 times the safe level of mercury on multiple doctor's visits, what do you think is going to happen to a young child's central nervous system? How about mercury poisoning.

Mercury Poisoning. Mercury poisoning is identical to Autism....IDENTICAL!

The supporters of the Pharmaceutical industry at the political, scientific and media levels have put a clever spin on this topic. They say that their products don't cause Autism. They are absolutely right. Their products cause MERCURY POISONING!

The Pharmaceutical Company's would love to get people into that argument because they know full well that Autism cannot be quantified in legal or medical terms at this time. They will win in court every time. These company's manipulated the statute of limitations rule in their vaccine courts. Their strategic planners did a great job.

If a suit ever does get a fair hearing, the parents will have one hell of a job in proving Autism. Every one of these suits that are pending should completely remove the word AUTISM. They need to insert the words MERCURY POISONING.

Let's ask a few basic questions regarding this mercury poisoning issue.

1) Did children's vaccines contain Thimerosal before 1999?

2) Does Thimerosal contain 49.6% mercury?

3) Did children receive vaccines that exposed them to levels of mercury that exceeded EPA levels by as much as 40 times?

4) Is mercury a deadly poison?

5) Why was mercury INTENTIONALLY injected into our children?

Literally thousands of parents have received the terrible answers to these questions in the form of a "mercury" brain damaged child. Statistics and cold, hard facts do not lie!

Unfortunately, these people are now a burden to our government.

Faced with these facts, the pharmaceutical industry needed a way to make this problem go away. The federal government was their answer. As a result, the government tried to roll this national tragedy into their National Security agenda and sweep this under the carpet. No other industry in America has this kind of governmental protection. WHY?

Is it because of the political donations? The financial gifts? President Bush's father sat on the Eli Lilly Board of directors?

Or perhaps of the stock ownership by governmental personnel in the pharmaceutical industry? Whatever the reason is, mercury poisoning thousands of innocent children is a national tragedy. This will not just go away. The fight has just begun and this issue will get very ugly. People are not just going to let this atrocity be swept away by a questionable national security issue.

It is very interesting that both Bush administrations have had Eli Lilly people right along side each President. President Bush (Vice President Quayle, Lilly's favorite son) and President Bush of today (Sidney Taurel and Mitch Daniels) It seems that Eli Lilly was and still is well represented in both Bush administrations.

Well, this sounds interesting, does it stick? And, will it hold up in court?

According to our In God we Trust Government, We may never know that answer.

Remember the statute of limitations in vaccine court? Three years!

After three years, the case is automatically dismissed, and since one must go through the vaccine court first……Sorry! The powerful special interests did it again, or did they?

Since the vaccine injury law was enacted to protect the pharmaceutical company's at the federal level and that the statute of limitations is only three years, that means that equal justice in the vaccine court cannot ever possibly be served in these cases. This means that the **Constitutional Amendments** 7 & 14 have been clearly violated.

The injured people have it within their power to contact their state Attorney Generals office and have them file a

criminal complaint against the Pharmaceutical companies who intentionally poisoned their children. This is a criminal complaint not a civil complaint. A state Attorney Generals office can file this type of complaint. If you knowingly cause injury to another person, then this is a criminal assault.

The statute of limitations must be expanded to the seven year rule. The injured parties need to contact their State Attorney Generals office and raise absolute hell.

Many State Attorney Generals offices in the past have made big differences in protecting the people within their states jurisdiction from illegal or harmful activity.

The State Attorney Generals offices in many states were the main reason the tobacco law suits were settled in court.

Since this is clearly criminal, the vaccine injury courts jurisdiction is superceded by the criminal court system. After the criminal proceedings, these cases would then go to the civil courts for monetary judgment. These vaccine courts clearly have no place in this due process.

The Vaccine Injury Act was enacted for only the vaccine it self. The additive, Thimerosal was never intended to be covered under this act, because if it would have, **the pharmaceutical company's would have had an obligation to the public to disclose this additive.** The pharmaceutical company's NEVER disclosed and people obviously would have objected to putting mercury into their babies. Again, **this is important**, the Government and the Pharmaceutical Company's **never** disclosed this dangerous additive to the parents of these damaged children. Failure to disclose a toxic substance or poison in an injected or ingested product for human consumption is clearly a felony offense. This also violates numerous consumer protection laws. Mr. Ralph Nader would love this case!

According to the Constitution of the United States of America, these children MUST have their day in court and that they MUST have equal protection under the law.

The GOP and the Pharmaceutical Industry will loose on these points in the Supreme Court. In fact, the whole vaccine injury court is UN Constitutional. It favors the few and takes away from the injured and because of the three year statute rule, this is also obstruction of justice. No one has of yet has brought this before the Supreme Court. It is time for action, NOW! The vaccine courts must be abolished. These courts are completely UNCONSTITUTIONAL because honest and fair justice can never be served in these courts.

The Supreme Courts job is to interpret and enforce the laws of the Constitution. Our supreme law of the land. It is unconscionable to deny equal rights to these injured children. The Supreme Court will rule in favor of these children.... and according to the Constitution, They MUST!

Late in 2002, The White House either knowingly or accidentally blew this whole thing wide open when they had their justice department file a motion to "seal" CDC documentation as it relates to the Thimerosal issue in children's vaccines. In 2000, the CDC did a study that indeed confirms that thimerosal causes brain damage.

The data presented in this report clearly demonstrated a 2.48 times greater chance of a child developing brain damage when a child is injected with the thimerosal that was used in the same quantities as was in the recommended vaccines that these children received on multiple doctor's visits over a period of sixteen months.

As a result of this study, the CDC ordered this report **confidential** and it was subsequently buried. The CDC had this prior knowledge. This has been proven by subpoenaed documents.

The innovative and clearly superior parents and organizations that are trying to get to the bottom of this issue, used the Freedom of Information Act to acquire this CDC report. BRAVO!

This reports confirmed everyone's worst fears…. it was the mercury.

The report also is great news…..Here's why………….

1)   Mercury poisoning can be proven in Court. It is not some obscure condition.

2)   Mercury poisoning if caught early enough can be treated.

3)   Since Mercury was intentionally added to the vaccines, damages can be qualified and quantified.

Here is the current legal and political status of what is happening at the present time.....

In November of 2002, the White House had Dick Armey (R. Texas) put in a last minute provision into the Homeland Security bill that protects the pharmaceutical company's specifically from thimerosal litigation. Under the new current law, a civil court action will be forced into the vaccine court.

Since the statute of limitations had already expired in the vaccine court, equal justice can never be served. Therefore, when the Homeland Security Act passed, this provision shut down ALL potential litigation in both court systems. As a result, the plaintiff will not be able to appeal the vaccine courts decision or even file a first complaint in the civil court system, and since they had already lost in vaccine court because of the three year statute, this provision effectively killed any chance of justice in either court. This was carefully planned by the powerhouse legal teams defending these cases. This is illegal, immoral, prejudice and it is UNCONSTITUTIONAL.

As a result of this special interest maneuver, the pharmaceutical industry's liability was exposed for everyone to see.

Why did the White House do this? Did they really think that this would go unnoticed? According to recent news reports, Bush's White House and Homeland security staff does indeed employ Mr. Sidney Taurel and Mr. Mitch Daniels.

Both of these gentlemen are current and past Lilly senior executives….. Interesting…..The plot gets thicker.

Does the White House think that they are so powerful that they can do this and the hell with everyone else? Of course not. They knew or should have known that there would be a fire storm of controversy and there was.

The Governments hand is exposed and it's as dirty as anything ever seen.

The pharmaceuticals power over the government has also been exposed.
Next, we will see a lot of paper shredding and the usual "I don't recalls".

This simple act revealed the truth that not only did the government and the pharmaceutical company's know that there was danger in these vaccines but it also told that there was a conspiracy and a cover up. Remember the CDC documented report that was buried? The government knew the truth and concealed it for many years. This is a criminal act and must be prosecuted.

Since the vaccine court is unconstitutional because it illegally denies the rights of the injured. All prior claims that have been denied by this unconstitutional vaccine court must be re instated and immediately filed in the proper criminal jurisdiction.

Experts agree that the cost of raising a "mercury damaged" child will exceed $ 3 million USD in the course of their lifetimes. The maximum amount you can receive in the so called vaccine court of justice is $ 250,000, plus costs.

And that's even if you do by some miracle, win a judgment. The parents of a mercury child are finding out that health insurance companies won't cover this type of injury because of a pre existing condition and to make matters worse, the costs of medical treatments have sky rocked. This medical burden has killed these working families. They have been financially wiped out.

Do the parents of a pharmaceutically damaged child have a problem? Who will pay? Why even bother with the vaccine court. This is why the White House put the special interest provision in the Homeland Security Bill. They knew that civil litigation was coming and they wanted to protect their "friends" and their campaign contributions.

This is now a criminal matter and must be treated as such. The people, who's children have been damaged need help. The executive branch of this government and the pharmaceutical industry that poisoned these children obviously doesn't give a damn.

All informed governmental personnel and their agencies who knew about this cover up must be subpoenaed and charged with conspiracy.

All Pharmaceutical company executives who profited from the increased sales from these thimerosal injections into our injured children (that were mandated by the government as necessary) must be held fiscally responsible for this tragedy. They illegally profited from the destruction of these children's brains. The government knew the risks and did absolutely nothing. In fact, they have attempted to cover this up and then send these suits to their illegal vaccine courts. This in essence is obstruction of justice…a felony! Our government, a felon? Should an investigation be started?

Meanwhile, in the lost world of the afflicted children, progress is being made with CHELATION (key-lation) treatments. Chelation is a heavy metal detoxification protocol that effectively removes metal from the brain tissues by being able to cross the blood-brain barrier and remove this poison.

During the denial process, the pharmaceutical company's consistently said that the tests that were done showed "no mercury in the blood samples".

Every physician in the world knows that Mercury accumulates in tissues, NOT IN THE BLOOD! Another lie and miss-direction on the part of the guilty. They published this information on the world wide web sights.

It is interesting to note that if you visit any of the governmental vaccine web sights, you will always find flowers, birds or children playing in a circle or something that looks like a children's doctors office. All of these sights categorically deny any damage from the vaccines.

Included in these web sights you will find the **updated version** of the vaccine content guide that shows very little Thimerosal in the current vaccines. This is further deception, because the vaccines in question need to be presented as **they actually were when these thousands of children received this poison between the years of 1986 and 1999 and even before that time**.

This is the one report that they don't want you to see.

These web sights always refer to the CDC report that denies the damage and they always say that there is no proof.

Well, The CDC report they refer to, is the report that was intentionally altered by the hired guns who re-printed this report to fit the pharmaceutical industries needs. This has been proven by subpoenas and internal investigations by Congressman Dan Burton. (R. Indiana)

During their investigations, Burton's committee found that all of the research people whose research was obviously a bias in favor of the pharmaceutical industry, were actually paid by the pharmaceutical industry to do this research.

I guess these people know what side their bread is buttered on. This is further evidence that one cannot possibly believe anything these people are saying. They also say that the chelation treatments are not advisable.

They must know that the chelation therapy will remove the mercury and they are obviously afraid of what the test results will be.

The chelation treatment is either in the form of DMSA, which is a capsule or DMPS which is an injection (that does not contain thimerosal) these two treatments are extremely helpful in removing the mercury from your child's brain TISSUES.

After 10 days to two weeks of treatment, the physician can do a stool test and a urine test.....The results are incredible. HEAVY METAL POISONING and in a documented form..... MERCURY!!!!!

After several treatments, parents are noticing huge improvements in the social and motor behaviors in their children. It's like their child's brain is waking up from a mercury sleep. Only time will tell if the damage is permanent. However, extensive damage has been done and no court in an honest and just society can deny these injured children their Constitutional Rights to bring a legal suit to trial against the makers of these mercury laden vaccines.

To look at an innocent child that has been the most assaulted and most innocent victim in medical history is enough to make even the most hardened mind cry in pain.

The people behind the manufacturing, packaging, distribution and cover up of this mercury tragedy must be punished and monetary awards must be awarded. The behaviors of the pharmaceutical industry and that of the U.S. government are inexcusable and are criminal.

The asbestos industry and the tobacco industry paid the price. Now the pharmaceutical industry MUST pay for its mistakes. They knew it and they conspired with the U.S. government to cover this all up.

The United Kingdom is seeing similar rates of "autism" The good people of the U.K. have figured this out as well. The Pharmaceutical Industry is just as powerful there as they are in the U.S., which leads me to an interesting point...

How come "autism" is skyrocketing only in the U.S and the U.K.?

This is because the two governments and the drug company's vaccinate their children in exactly the same way. No other country does this. As a result, NO brain damage in children in these other countries. Look at the facts and do the research. This however is beginning to change.

The press, at the urging of some good people is starting to finely report on this tragedy, too much has happened. The word has finely gotten out. People want answers. Now the presses are starting to roll, great! I have found articles that point the way to justice. This will take time. Remember, the pharmaceutical company's are very rich and very powerful. Since the U.S. government is in their corner, this is almost an unbeatable combination. Only the avenue of truth and UN bias exposure will make this a fair, legal fight. Public opinion and public awareness will cause needed transparency in this industry.

I am not anti government nor am I anti vaccines. I am anti crime, and what these particular people did in this particular industry is criminal. The whole U.S. government cannot be blamed for this cover up nor can the whole pharmaceutical industry be blamed. There are good and honest people in government and in the pharmaceutical industry that must feel the same way as the parents of these children feel... Betrayed and lied to.

I am a truth seeker in this. I think it would be in everyone's best interest to have the governmental people that are involved as well as the pharmaceutical people involved, lay their cards out and be honest. A terrible tragedy has occurred. It's time to face the music and stop lying and smoke screening the truth.

Below are some recent articles on the vaccine injury issue.

Autism and Mercury

By Permission
> by Tim O'Shea, DC

This article is excerpted from Dr. O'Shea's revised edition of The Sanctity of Human Blood.

Inquiry into vaccine safety is exploding like never before, even in the popular press. Research coming from dozens of mainstream medical studies can no longer be easily suppressed, as it has been in the past, especially with the prevalence of online information exchange.

Last September, some 2,000 people, mostly MDs, assembled at the Town and Country resort in San Diego to hear the latest research on autism. Following the April 2000 Congressional hearings on autism and vaccines, this epidemic can no longer be ignored.

The figure of one autistic infant for every 150 is now widely documented.

Dr. Stephanie Cave presented enlightening data on mercury toxicity, drawn largely from the brilliant work of Sallie Bernard. Dr. Cave explained how:

By age two, American children have received 237 micrograms of mercury through vaccines alone, which far exceeds current EPA "safe" levels of .1 mcg/kg. per day. That's one-tenth of a microgram, not one microgram.

Three days in particular may be singled out as spectacularly toxic for infants:

Day of birth: hepatitis B-12 mcg mercury

20 x safe level

At 4 months: DTaP and HiB on same day – 50 mcg mercury

60 x safe level

At 6 months: Hep B, Polio – 62.5 mcg mercury

78 x safe level

at 15 months the child receives another 50 mcg

41 x safe level

These figures are calculated for an infant's average weight in kilograms for each age.

These one-day blasts of mercury are called "bolus doses". Although they far exceed "safe" levels, there has never been any research conducted on the toxicity of such bolus doses of mercury given to infants all these years.

Inconceivable

Historically, the toxicity of mercury has been known for more than a century. The Mad Hatter was more than a fantasy character from Alice in Wonderland. Mad Hatter's disease became well known in England in the mid-1800s, when hat-makers were subject to inhaling the vapors from the mercury-based stiffening compound they used on felt to make top hats.

Sources of Mercury

It is interesting to learn that common household remedies that were used up into the 1960s like mercurochrome and "teething powder" were often the cause of acute mercury poisoning and disease.

In the U.S., EPA mercury toxicity studies have involved contamination from fish, air, and other environmental sources.

Methylmercury long been associated with serious neurological disorders, demyelinating diseases, gut disease, and visual damage.

The mercury in vaccines, however, is in the form of thimerosal, which is 50 times more toxic than plain old mercury.

Reasons for this include:

- **Injected mercury is far more toxic than ingested mercury.**
- **There's no blood-brain barrier in infants.**
- **Mercury accumulates in brain cells and nerves.**

• **Infants don't produce bile, which is necessary to excrete mercury.**

Thimerosal becomes organic mercury

Once it is in nerve tissue, it is converted irreversibly to its inorganic form. Thimerosal is a much more toxic form of mercury than one would get from eating open-sea fish; it has to do with the difficulty of clearing thimerosal from the blood.

Thimerosal is converted to ethylmercury, an organic form that has a preference for nerve cells.

Without a complete blood-brain barrier, an infant's brain and spinal cord are sitting ducks. Once in the nerve cells, mercury is changed back to theinorganic form and becomes tightly bound. Mercury can then remain for years, like a time-release capsules, causing permanent degeneration and death of brain cells.

Bernard also notes that the body normally clears mercury by fixing it to bile, but before six months of age, infants don't produce bile. Result: **mercury can't be excreted.**

Four separate government agencies have set safe levels for methylmercury, but no safe levels have ever been set for thimerosal, because thimerosal isn't included in toxicity studies.

Theoretically, that means that the above excesses of safe levels of mercury on the single days listed above are actually 50 times higher.

Does the fact that the mercury is accompanied by a vaccine somehow place it above scrutiny? The Sallie Bernard study of vaccines and mercury toxicity was probably the main reason Congress began to see the obvious correlation.

Mercury And Vaccines

Here's a curious "coincidence." In the late 1930s, Leo Kanner identified autism as a new type of mental disorder. So when was thimerosal introduced into vaccines?

The 1930s

A few years ago, Bernard and her associates began to notice a striking similarity between the symptoms of autism and the symptoms of mercury poisoning. The more research she did, the more it seemed that these two diseases were virtually identical.

Autism and mercury poisoning damage the: brain/nerve cells; eyes; immune system; gastrointestinal system; muscle control; and the speech center.

Although mercury toxicity has been studied for decades, and EPA safety levels have been set, during all that time a child's greatest exposure to mercury – thimerosal in vaccines – was never even included in the toxicity studies!

The talk has always been about methylmercury from seafood and the environment, totally ignoring the two most toxic sources of mercury for children: vaccines and dental amalgams.

The EPA has no jurisdiction over drugs.

That's the FDA's job. This is why vaccines and amalgams don't even figure into the equation when it comes to setting "safe" levels of mercury.

But the FDA does have jurisdiction over drugs and drug companies, right? And over drug company publications, like the Merck Manual, the standard cookbook for drugs and diseases found in every doctor's office in the world.

Surely the FDA, as the government agency charged with safeguarding the nation's health, would want the section on mercury toxicity to warn doctors about the two biggest sources for children: thimerosal and dental amalgams, wouldn't you think?

Yet looking at the Merck Manual (1999), in the section on mercury poisoning (p. 2636), thimerosal and dental amalgams again are not even mentioned!

How can this be, when mercury is widely acknowledged as the third most deadly toxin in the world and thimerosal and amalgams dwarf the trace amounts of mercury from fish and other environmental sources of mercury?

Only one thing can a blackout information over an entire area of study for years at a time in this way – **big money.**

Such an omission probably wouldn't have anything to do with the revolving door that exists between the FDA; the EPA; the NIH;

"and the sweet positions held by their members before and after those grueling years of public service; or with the 800 waivers of the conflict of interest rule that the FDA has granted in the past two years to "experts," who are paid consultants to the drug companies-consultants who are also members of the FDA advisory committees that make decisions about whether or not to approve vaccines and drugs..." (USA Today, Sept. 25, 2000)

No, of course not.

Soaking up the Mercury

In the San Diego conference on autism, Dr. Amy Holmes gave perhaps the only lucid presentation about treatment. She explained how chelating drugs alone, which go through the blood like Pac Man munching up mercury, don't do much good for autism.

That's because most mercury clears from the blood very soon. Mercury in thimerosal is stored in the gut, liver and brain, and as previously mentioned, becomes very tightly bound to the cells. Once inside those cells, or inside the blood-brain barrier, the mercury is reconverted back to its inorganic form.

Locked into these cells, the mercury can then do either immediate cell damage or become latent and cause the onset of autism, brain disorders, or digestive chaos years later.

Dr. Holmes reported success using alphalipoic acid as an agent to cross the blood-brain barrier to soak up mercury. Once the mercury is brought back into the bloodstream, standard chelators like DMSA can then take it out.

Dr. Holmes has used her protocol on about 300 autistics so far, and shows consistent increases in IQ scores.

FDA: Protector of Whom?

In the face of all this new awareness, it was astounding that in July 2000 the FDA came out with the "parallel-Universe" pronouncement that "vaccines have safe levels of mercury."

Especially after their 1998 position:

"…over-the-counter drug products containing thimerosal and other mercury forms are not generally recognized as safe and effective."

As if there were any doubt as to who's really running the show, inconceivable also is the impotence of FDA's request to the vaccine manufacturers to discontinue the use of thimerosal in vaccines (LINK TO ARTICLE ON SITE) The same month that MMWR published this, the CDC made the same milquetoast request.

It's a bit like saying: "Hey guys, since all these kids are turning into vegetables and most of our researchers know it's the mercury, would you mind not putting any more thimerosal in your vaccines, please? No hurry, though. Whenever you're ready. No need to dump all those batches of vaccine just because people are finding out it's the mercury that's destroying children's brain cells."

The members of the FDA who decide which vaccines get approved make up the advisory board. In his recent House investigation on vaccines, Rep. Dan Burton found out that financial statements of advisory board members are "incomplete."

Noting that this is the only branch of government that allows incomplete financials, in September 2000, Burton called the advisory board's sweetheart arrangements with the vaccine manufacturers a "violation of the public trust."

This includes 70 percent of advisory board members owning stock in vaccines, owning patents on vaccines, and accepting salaries and benefits as employees of the drug companies.

A Matter of Trust

Still think you can trust the government or your physician with your children's blood? Despite the facts and events cited above, consider this joint statement of the U.S. Public Health Services and the American Academy of Pediatrics:

"There is a significant safety margin incorporated into all the acceptable mercury exposure limits. There are no data or evidence of any harm caused by the level of exposure that some children may have encountered in following the existing immunization schedule ... Infants and children who have received thimerosal-containing vaccines do not need to be tested for mercury exposure" (TRY TO REPLACE THIS WITH LINK FROM SITE MMWR, vol. 45, 1999).

These are blatant Orwellian distortions. No harm?

- **What about the autism epidemic and all the evidence linking it with mercury cited above?**
- **What about the single day doses of mercury cited above that are dozens of times in excess of the EPA's own safety levels?**
- **If everything is so safe, then why did they ask the vaccine pushers to kindly discontinue thimerosal from vaccines as soon as possible at the end of this same statement?**

It is beyond the scope of this paper to really go into the politics of mercury. In researching mercury toxicity, a whole area of "dry rot" has been unearthed that deserves its own story. This is the shocking story of how the American Dental Association and the California Dental Association have been systematically hiding the truth about mercury toxicity in fillings for decades.

Silver fillings aren't just silver. They're 50 percent mercury and extremely toxic; every dentist knows it (www.altcorp.com,http://www.amalgam.org/).

In a ludicrous blast of irony, both the ADA and the CDA have inserted into their "code of ethics" strict commandments forbidding dentists from every revealing to patients the realities of mercury toxicity.

No dentist is allowed to recommend removal of mercury amalgams for health reasons, nor may tell the patient about mercury toxicity even if the patient asks. This gag order has been in place for since the beginning of American dentistry. Exaggeration? Check their websites out:

www.amalgam.org/#anchor69176   www. amalgam.org/ #anchor69541

Do you think dentists put mercury into their own families' teeth? Ask them. Anyone who is not a dentist is not constrained by the gag order, imposed on American dentists by the ADA, against telling patients what many perceptive researchers in the field of mercury toxicity already know: that no children should ever get mercury amalgam fillings.

Laughingstock of the West

Researchers across Europe are generally appalled at the massive amounts of vaccines given to American children under two years old. Although Europeans are not as obsessed with vaccines as we are, they do vaccinate.

But most of Europe gives very few vaccinations to children under two years old, primarily because of the unformed gut, immune system, and blood-brain barrier.

This intellectual isolation of ours regarding vaccines is a testimony to the suffocating "brain control" exerted on us by the popular press and all media. Like sheep to the slaughter, we don't know enough to be appalled by our own ignorance.

Autistic Gut

Headlining the September 2000 San Diego Conference was Andrew Wakefield, the British surgeon whose shocking new discoveries show that mercury toxicity alone is not the only factor linking vaccines with the autism epidemic. Dr. Wakefield's research centers around the MMR vaccine – measles/mumps/rubella – which does not contain thimerosal.

Expanding on his presentation at the April 2000 Burton hearings, Dr. Wakefield explained how at least three-quarters of autistics have pathologically blocked bowels, due to the huge swelling of the tissue lining the intestine.

In virtually every autistic patient they examined, this nodular hyperplasia is both an immune response and an autoimmune response that Wakefield and O'Leary have clearly linked to the presence of measles virus from the MMR shot. No other virus was found in those cells.

It is a new bowel pathology.

Wakefield showed graphs of the U.S. and U.K. 10 years apart that were identical in tracing the skyrocketing incidence of autism just after the MMR vaccine was introduced.

He also showed how the incidence of measles had dropped over 85 percent on its own before the MMR was introduced.

One incredible study cited by Wakefield showed how 76 percent of children whose mothers were exposed to atypical measles became autistic after the MMR shot! He called this a "background susceptibility" or predisposition to autism.

Wakefield reminds us that in neither country have there ever been comparative studies on giving multiple vaccines (polyvalent) on the same day.

This custom of ours, with both the DPT and the MMR, is not scientific by any stretch, and is primarily for the convenience of those administering the shots, and those being paid per vaccine. As a result, there is a good chance of geometric ill effects.

Then Wakefield cited the original MMR study (Buynak, Journal of the American Medical Association 1969, vol. 207).

Not only was the safety of multiple vaccines never mentioned, there was no follow-up to the study to see if their conclusions were correct.

In the usual manner of testing vaccines on the live population, MMR was simply tacked onto the mandatory schedule, and we've never looked back.

Despite studies in 1981 on Air Force personnel showing major synergistic adverse effects in the gut from the combination of measles and rubella vaccines, the mandatory schedule went unchanged.

A Glimmer of Hope

Despite these formidable obstacles, doubts are creeping into the overall public "consciousness" about the safety of vaccines. At one in 150, the fact of autism as an epidemic can no longer be covered up.

The work of Wakefield, O'Leary, Megson and Bernard is getting more and more difficult to explain away. Rep. Dan Burton seems relentless in his efforts to acquaint Congress with the meretricious relationship between the FDA Advisory Committee and the vaccine manufacturers.

The massive advertising campaign about the safety of vaccines in the popular media, which is certain to be stepped up in the next few months, is going to look very hollow in the light of clean, unbiased research that is not funded by parties who stand to make billions from certain predetermined results.

And the internet makes this well-referenced, scientific work accessible to the public without the usual monodimensional smokescreen from the popular press.

Ultimately, the value of the San Diego "Conference on Autism" was its signal that autism will not be allowed to slip from the public awareness, like so many other feature stories that come and go. The simple truth has been unveiled, and anyone who looks can see it clearly: our prime question should not be asking how we can cure autism once it occurs. The evidence is now overwhelming that in most cases, this new epidemic that we can autism is a preventable disease.

http://www.thedoctorwithin,com/

DR. MERCOLA'S COMMENT:

Congratulations to Dr. O'Shea for an excellent review of this important topic.

Related Articles:

Autism and Mercury Detoxification

Autism: a Novel Form of Mercury Poisoning

Studies on the Effects of Secretin in Children With Autism

Single Injection Of Secretin Does Not Treat Autism

Objections to the Study That Showed Secretin Does Not Work for Autism

Short-term Benefit In Treating Autism With Antibiotics

The Neurobiology of Lipids In Autistic Spectrum Disorder

Link Between Autism and Vaccination

Autism May Be Caused By an Immune System Response To a Virus

Vaccine – Autism Link Feared

Vaccine Induced Autism

Milk Link to Autism

References:

Halsey N. Limiting infant exposure to thimerosal in vaccines. JAMA 1999;282:1763.

Cave S. Lecture, DAN 2000 Conference 15 Sept. 2000 San Diego.

Shattock P. Lecture DAN 2000 Conference 15 Sept. 2000 Dan Diego.

Crawford. MMR in Air Force personnel. Journal of Infectious Disease 1981;144:403.

Bristol M., et al. State of the science in autism: report to the National Institutes of Health Journal of Autism and Developmental Disorders 1996;26 (2):121-157.

McGinnis W. Lecture, DAN 200 Conference, San Diego, 16 Sep 00.

AAP/USPHS joint statement about the safety of thimerosal in vaccines Morbidity and Mortality Weekly Report 1999;48:563.

Bernard S., et al. Autism: a unique type of mercury poisoning – ARC Research, April 3, 2000 (http://www.autism.com/ari/mercurylong.html).

Pilgrim W., et al. Proceedings of the Conference on Mercury in Eastern Canada and the Northeast States, University of Quebec 1998. (http://www.cciw.ca/eman-temp/reports/publications/98_mercury2/).

Dr. Nathan's baby growth chart. (http://www.babyzone.com/drnathan/medref/growthchart.htm).

Buynak E. Combined live measles, mumps, and rubella virus vaccines JAMA March 1969;207(12):2259.

Cauchon D. FDA advisers tied to industry. USA Today, September 2000, page one.

Spitzer W. Department of Epidemiology & Biostatistics, McGill University. c-span.org – Government Reform Committee Hearing on Vaccines and Autism, 6 Apr 2000, Chairman: Representative Dan Burton.

The Merck Manual, 17th edition, Merck Research Labs, 1999.

Morbidity and Mortality Weekly Report, 9 July 1999, April 2000. Howell, Edward. Enzyme Nutrition. 1985 Avery.

Price W. Nutrition and Physical Degeneration. 1939 Keats.

Tilden JH. Toxemia Explained. 1926 Kessinger.

Lee R. Conversations in Nutrition Standard Process. 1955.

Wiley H. The Foods and Their Adulterations. 1930.

www.thedoctrowithin.com.

Tim O'Shea,DC San Jose, California
http://www.chiroweb.com/archives/19/05/02.htm

Courtney L. Zietzke

Privacy/Security Current Newsletter Contact Info

Disclaimer – Newsletters are based upon the opinions of Dr. Mercola. They are not intended to replace a one-on-one relationship with a qualified health care professional and they are not intended as medical advice. They are intended as a sharing of knowledge and information from the research and experience of Dr. Mercola and his community. Dr. Mercola encourages you to make your own health care decisions based upon your research and in partnership with a qualified health care professional.

Vaccines fueling autism epidemic?

Report: U.S. infants exposed to mercury beyond EPA, FDA limits

---

Posted: June 9, 2003
5:00 p.m. Eastern   **By Permission**

Editor's note: WorldNetDaily is pleased to have a content-sharing agreement with Insight magazine, the bold Washington publication not afraid to ruffle establishment feathers. Subscribe to Insidhe at WorldNetDaily's online store and save 71 percent off the cover price.

By Kelly Patricia O Meara
© 2003 News World Communications Inc.

The mother of an autistic child wonders aloud when health officials will wake up to the epidemic that has claimed not only her son but hundreds of thousands of other children in the United States, with no end in sight. She muses, "Maybe someday this will be as important as SARS and we'll get the same attention. God knows we need it."

Autism is a severely incapacitating developmental disability for which there is no known cure. According to a recently released report by the California Department of Developmental Services, or DDS, entitled Autistic Spectrum Disorders, Changes in the California Caseload: 1999-2002, the rate of children diagnosed with full-syndrome autism in the Golden State between 1999 and 2002 nearly doubled from

10,360 to 20,377. The report further revealed that "between Dec. 31, 1987, and Dec. 31, 2002, the population of persons with full-syndrome autism has increased by 634 percent." That is a doubling of autism cases every four years, and the staggering increases are not limited to California.

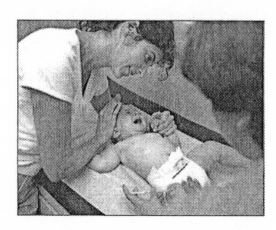

"
Maybe
*someday
this will be
as important
as SARS
and we'll
get the
same
attention.*
***God knows
we need it.***

—*Mother of
autistic
child*

Infants are being inoculated with vaccines containing toxic ingredients that can be harmful – or fatal.

(This caption was placed below the picture in the original.) According to data provided by the U.S. Department of Education, the increased autism rate in California is in line with the increases other states are experiencing. For example, in 1992 Ohio reported 22 cases. A decade later the number had increased by 13,895 percent to 3,057. In Illinois the rate of autism cases climbed from just five in 1992 to 3,802 – an increase of 76,040 percent.

Mississippi, New Hampshire and the District of Columbia reported no cases of autism in 1992, but by 2002 the number of cases reported were 461, 404 and 144, respectively.

Only Puerto Rico can claim to have an increase of less than 100 percent, with the remaining states reporting increases of at least 500 percent during the same period.

A recently published study in the Journal of American Physicians and Surgeons by Mark Geier, M.D., Ph.D., and president of the Genetic Centers of America and his son, David Geier, president of Medcon Inc. and a consultant on vaccine cases, was titled "Thimerosal in Childhood Vaccines, Neurodevelopment Disorders and Heart Disease in the United States." It presents strong epidemiological evidence for a link between neurodevelopmental disorders and mercury exposure from thimerosal-containing childhood vaccines.

Specifically, the authors evaluated the doses of mercury that children received as part of their immunization schedule, then compared these doses with federal safety guidelines. Furthermore, to compare the effects of thimerosal in vaccine recipients, the incident rates of neurodevelopmental disorders and heart disease reported to the government's Vaccine Adverse Events Reporting System were analyzed. The results were dramatic. The report revealed that "U.S. infants are exposed to mercury levels from their childhood-immunization schedule that far exceed the EPA [Environmental Protection Agency] and FDA [Food and Drug Administration]-established maximum permissible levels for the daily oral ingestion of methyl mercury."

The authors concluded that "in light of voluminous literature supporting the biologic mechanisms for mercury-induced adverse reactions, the presence of amounts of mercury in thimerosal-containing childhood vaccines exceeding federal safety guidelines for the oral ingestion of mercury and previous epidemiological studies showing adverse reactions to such vaccines, a causal relationship between thimerosal-containing childhood vaccines and neurodevelopment disorders and heart disease appears to be confirmed."

It is no secret among government and health officials that mercury is toxic and causes serious adverse reactions. In July 1999 the American Academy of Pediatrics and the U.S. Public Health Service issued a joint statement calling for the removal of thimerosal from vaccines. Five years after the joint statement, however, it still is difficult for parents and physicians to be sure that the pharmaceutical companies have indeed removed the toxic substance from their vaccines.

According to Mark Geier, "The 2003 Physicians' Desk Reference, or PDR, still shows childhood vaccines containing thimerosal, including diphtheria, tetanus and acellular pertussis. DTaP, manufactured by Aventis Pasteur, contains 25µ [25 micrograms] of mercury, Hemophilus influenzae b (Hib) vaccine manufactured by Wyeth contains 25µg of mercury and pediatric Hepatitis B vaccine, manufactured by Merck, contains 12.5µg of mercury."

Geier continues, "In addition, the influenza vaccine that is recommended for an increasing segment of the pediatric population in the U.S. also contains 25µg of mercury. Assuming that the labeling is correct, it is possible that children in the U.S. in 2003 may be exposed to levels of mercury from thimerosal contained in childhood vaccines that are at higher levels than at any time in the past. Possible total childhood mercury in 2003 is more than 300µg."

Whether the "labeling is correct" is the question du jour. According to Len Lavenda, a spokesman for Aventis Pasteur, the maker of DTaP, "Aventis only sells the DTaP vaccine in the preservative-free formulation. The PDR references both the single and multidose. However, when we received the license for the preservative-free we ceased sales of the multidose vial. For some reason, the package insert takes much longer to revise than one would expect. I believe it is at the FDA waiting for approval, but the fact is we do not sell or market that product. In March 2001 we stopped all sales of that product in the preservative formulation. We did not recall the product at that time because it was our belief that if we did children may go unimmunized. It's been two years since anyone has been able to purchase the preservative formulation from us."

Lavenda continues: "The package insert talks about both the single and multidose vials and it says that the single-dose vial is preservative-free, and that is all that is sold. The PDR is outdated, but parents don't have to worry about their children being administered 25µg of thimerosal. It just takes time to get the paperwork caught up. The current package insert does not accurately reflect what is being marketed."

Geier is astounded by Lavenda's admission. "If this is true, they should be in jail. They can't have an insert on a drug that is totally wrong. It is against all regulations. If I'm a doctor and I'm giving you a shot and the insert says such and such is in the shot, it had better be in it. If doctors can't rely on the instructions that come with what we're injecting then all bets are off. This is a far worse admission than admitting that thimerosal is still in the vaccine. There are at least 15 laws that say the insert has to match what is in the product. This is absolutely horrendous. In my entire career in medicine I have never heard of a drug company claiming that what's in the insert and the accompanying produce don't match. This is total mislabeling and fraud by their own admission. Legally they should be forced to close down because our clinical decisions are based on their labeling."

Assuming that the package inserts are correct, Geier tells Insight, "The EPA limit is 0.1 micrograms of mercury per kilogram body weight per day. It doesn't take a genius to do the calculations when on their day of birth children are given the hepatitis B vaccine, which is 12.5 micrograms of mercury. The average newborn weighs between 6 and 7 pounds, so they would be allowed 0.3 micrograms of mercury – but in this one shot they are getting 12.5 micrograms. That's 39 times more than allowed by law. And it gets worse when you consider that children are getting multiple vaccinations at 2 months. And this limit is for oral ingestion and not injection, which is much worse."

Rhonda Smith, a spokeswoman for the federal Centers for Disease Control and Prevention, tells Insight that, except for mere traces, thimerosal has been removed. "All routinely recommended licensed vaccines," says Smith, "that are currently being manufactured for children in the U.S., except influenza, contain no thimerosal or only trace amounts – a concentration of less than 0.0002 percent." But according to the 2003 immunization schedule and the package inserts, there appear to be a number of childhood vaccines that still contain mercury, including those for tetanus and diphtheria.

This scenario becomes even more bizarre when one further considers that thimerosal is not a necessary component in vaccines. It first was introduced by pharmaceutical giant Eli Lilly and Co. in the 1930s and is added to vaccines only as a preservative – the theory being that multiple doses are taken from the same bottle and that thimerosal will protect against contamination. However, according to Geier, "the solution to any such problem is to make vaccines available in a single dose, which will cost the pharmaceuticals about one penny more. What is interesting is that if you look up the mumps, measles, rubella [MMR] vaccines in the PDR you'll see that they do not contain thimerosal because it would kill the live virus. The MMR is available in multidose packaging and, yet, there is no preservative – nothing. What they did was put a label on it that says 'This product does not contain preservatives. Handle with care.' It's that simple."

Geier insists, "I'm pro-vaccines, but the bottom line is that our kids are getting massive amounts of mercury. Mercury has been withdrawn from everything, including animal vaccines, yet we keep injecting it into our children. Everyone should absolutely refuse to take a vaccine shot that has thimerosal in it, and they should insist on reading the vaccine package insert. Our data showed that the more mercury children received in their childhood vaccines the more neurodevelopment disorders there are. We've looked at this every possible way and every time there's massive evidence to support it."

So, if everyone acknowledges the toxicity of mercury and top U.S. health officials have called for its removal, why is thimerosal still in vaccines?

"Maybe," concludes Geier, "the mercury isn't being taken out all at once because if the pharmaceutical companies did that you would see an unbelievable change in the rate of autism and there would be massive lawsuits. If you look at the graphs now they go up and up. If you stop the thimerosal all at once you'd see the numbers fall dramatically."

Rep. Dan Burton, R-Ind., a longtime advocate for victims of autism, has a grandson who became autistic after receiving nine vaccines in one day. Burton recently sent his second request in as many years to the White House asking for a conference of scientists, researchers and parents to look into the causes of autism.

The Indiana lawmaker tells Insight, "There is no doubt in my mind that the mercury in vaccines is a major contributing factor to a growing number of neurological disorders among children, but in particular autism."

Burton explains that "thimerosal is a toxic substance – mercury – and should not be put in close proximity of people, should not be injected into people, especially children who have a newly formed immune system that may not be able to handle it. To my knowledge there never have been long-term tests on thimerosal and we never should have used mercury in vaccines, period. Now what we've got is an epidemic that is absolutely out of control."

The Indiana congressman continues, "One reason this isn't getting the attention it needs is that the Food and Drug Administration has very close ties to the pharmaceutical companies, as does the Department of Health and Human Services [HHS] and the Centers for Disease Control. I've said in the past that in some cases it appears that it's a revolving door and people leave government health agencies and go to work for the pharmaceuticals, which I think have undue influence on our health agencies. Of course, they may not want to look at this because there's a possibility that large claims be filed and the pharmaceutical companies would have to cough up the money to take care of these kids who have been damaged."

Burton means business. He insists, "The FDFA, CDC and HHS should put out in a very public way the dangers of mercury, but as soon as they do it will amount to an admission that their mercury is causing these problems. So the reports that come out of the FDA, CDC and HHS use ambiguous terms. Well, if they're not sure, and there's the remotest possibility that mercury in vaccines could cause autism, they ought to get thimerosal off the market. Too many kids are being ruined for life because of this stuff.

Barbara Loe Fisher is founder of the National Vaccine Information Center, a charitable organization dedicated to the prevention of vaccine injuries and deaths through public education. Fisher tells Insight, "There are many things in vaccines that could be causing these disorders, and thimerosal is only part of the problem. In the last 20 years, we've gone from giving children 23 doses of seven vaccines to 38 doses of 12 vaccines. I think the mercury is part of it for some kids, though I'm not sure it's the answer for all." But this is a no-brainer, says Fisher. "Mercury shouldn't be in vaccines. They've taken it out of everything else so why not the vaccines? The one thing that people really need to look at is the dramatic rise in chronic disease and disabilities in our kids in just the last two decades. You have to admit that there is something occurring that a growing number of children cannot get through without being immune-system and brain-system damaged. And what is the one thing that we expose every child to? Those vaccines."

Fisher concludes, "I've always argued that public health is not measured only by an absence of infectious disease. It also is measured by the absence of chronic disease. By that score we get a big fat 'F.' So we don't have measles and mumps, but look what we have now. It's just really simple: Take the mercury out and let's see what happens."

Even so, based on the Aventis admission that the package insert does not reflect what is in the vaccine, it will be difficult to know when, if ever, thethimerosal actually has been removed. This skews the data about the relationship between thimerosal and autism. More important, it means parents cannot be sure the vaccinations their children receive are free of mercury.

Neither the Wyeth nor Merck pharmaceutical companies, nor HHS or FDS, returned Insight's calls about this matter.

Courtney L. Zietzke

AAA Wellness Today
by Permission

"A Better Way for a Better Life!"

Volume 5 Number 6 March 2003

Mercury-based vaccine preservative linked to
neurological injury to infants

By

Claire M. Bothwell
Waters & Kraus, LLP
200 Oceangate, Suite 520
Long Beach, California 90802
Tel: (562) 436-8833
Fax: (562) 590-7296

The Dallas-based law firm of Waters & Kraus announced today that it has received documents, as a result of the discovery process in the case of Counter v. Eli Lilly & Company, et al, currently pending in Brazoria County, Texas that come from the archives of Eli Lilly & Company. The documents clearly demonstrate that Lilly's thimerosal product, the mercury-based vaccine preservative implicated in a number of recent law suits, as causing neurological injury to infants, was known to be dangerous, as early as April 1930.

In its apparent eagerness to promote and market the product, in September, 1930, Eli Lilly secretly sponsored a "human toxicity" study on patients already known to be dying of meningococcal meningitis. Senior partner Andrew Waters stated that, "Lilly then cited this study repeatedly for decades as proof that thimerosal was of low toxicity and harmless to humans. They never revealed to the scientific community or the public the highly questionable nature of the original research."

While Eli Lilly made every effort to corrupt the medical and scientific literature, the process of arranging to publish the results of its questionable secret study, other researchers have provided Lilly with numerous articles since the 1930's indicating concerns about thimerosal and its potential hazard to humans who might be exposed or, injected with the substance.

The evidence clearly demonstrates that Eli Lilly was advised repeatedly that their conclusions of low toxicity were not warranted and that they failed to pass the information on to appropriate federal and public health authorities. The following time line illustrates some, but by no means all, of the documentary evidence on this point from Lilly's internal files:

1947 – Article received by Lilly: "No eruptions or reactions have been observed or reported to merthiolate internally, but it may be dangerous to inject a serum containing merthiolate into a patient sensitive to merthiolate."

1948 – Article received by Lilly: "Merthiolate is such a commonly used preservative for biologicals, plasma, cartilage, etc., that it would seem important to determine whether harm would result following its subcutaneous or intravenous injection in skin sensitive individuals."

1950 – New York Academy of Science article, "Mercurials as Antiseptics:"It(merthiolate)istoxicwheninjectedparenterally and; therefore, cannot be used in chemotherapy."

1963 – Article received by Lilly: "There is another point of practical significance: does the parenteral injection of merthiolate-containing fluids cause disturbances in merthiolate-sensitive patients?" "It is known that persons that are contact sensitive to a drug may tolerate the same medications internally, but it seems advisable to use a preservative other than merthiolate for injections in merthiolate-sensitive people."

8/17/67 – Medical/Science department requests that the claim "non-toxic" on thimerosal labels be deleted in next printing run.

8/29/67 – Draft label changed to "non-irritating to body tissues," non-toxic omitted.

1972 – British Medical Journal reports case of skin burns resulting from the chemical interaction of thimerosal and aluminum. "Mercury is known to act as a catalyst and to cause aluminum to oxidize rapidly, with the production of heat. "The manufacturers who supply us with thimerosal have been informed." [Thimerosal is being used in vaccines, which also contain aluminum].

1972 – Article received by Lilly: Merthiolate in vaccines cause six deaths? "The symptoms and clinical course of the six patients suggest subacute mercury poisoning."

4/27/76 – Lilly responds to Rexall Drug Company's efforts to place the following warning on Merthiolate product: "Frequent or prolonged use or application to large areas may cause mercury poisoning."

Lilly objects to this proposed warning, stating: "We object to the connection of our trademark with the unjustified alarm and concern on the part of the user which the statement is likely to cause? We are not aware of any instance of 'mercury poisoning' after decades of marketing this product. This is because the mercury in the product is organically bound ethyl mercury, as a completely non-toxic nature, not methyl mercury."

1/5/82 FDA's advance notice of proposed rule making regarding thimerosal:

"At the cellular level, thimerosal has been found to be more toxic for human epithelial cells in vitro than mercuric chloride, mercuric nitrate, and merbromim (mercurichrom). "It was found to be 35.3 times more toxic for embryonic chick heart tissue than for staphylococcus areas."

1950 study showed that thimerosal was no better than water in protecting mice from potential fatal streptococcal infection."

"The Panel concludes that thimerosal is not safe for OTC topical use because of its potential for cell damage if applied to broken skin and its allergy potential. It is not effective as a topical antimicrobial because its bacteria static action can be reversed."

4/7/83 – Additional language added to some Lilly labels: "As with any drug, if you are pregnant or nursing a baby, seek the advice of a health professionals before using this product."

1991 – Lilly ceases manufacture/sale of thimerosal. Licensing agreements demonstrate continued profits from the product until at least 2010.

12/8/99 Lilly MSDS regarding thimerosal: "Primary Physical & Reproduction Effects: Nervous System and Reproduction Effects"

"Effects of exposure include fetal changes.

"Mercury poisoning may occur."

"Exposure in children may cause mild to severe mental retardation... ."

"Hypersensitivity to mercury is a medical condition aggravated by exposure."

CERCLAL Hazardous substance? toxic waste disposal.

Waters & Kraus is litigating a growing number of individual cases across the country involving infants that sustained serious neurological injuries from the thimerosal contained in their pediatric vaccines. Waters & Kraus is leading the following coalition of firms in bringing these cases to trial:

Evert & Weathersby, L.L.C.
3405 Piedmont Road, Suite 225
Atlanta, Georgia 30305-1764
Tel: 404.233.8718

DORAN & MURPHY, LLP
1234 Delaware Avenue
Buffalo, New York 14209
Tel: 716.884.2000

Dogan & Wilkinson
726 Delmas Avenue
Pascagoula, Mississippi 39567
Tel: 228.762.2272

O'CONNELL & O'SULLIVAN
217 N. McLean Blvd., Suite 2C
Elgin, Illinois 60123
Tel: 847-741-4603

Hendrickson & Long
214 Capital Street
P.O. Bo 11070
Charleston, W. VA 25339

Courtney L. Zietzke
Tel: 304.346.5500

ANDERSON & KRIGER, APLC
40925 County Center Drive, Suite 210
Temecula, California 92591
Tel: 909.296.5090

WISE & JULIAN, PC
3555 College Avenue
Alton, Illinois 62002
Tel: 618.462.2600

MARTZELL & BICKFORD
338 Lafayette Street
New Orleans, Louisiana 70130
Tel: 504.581.9065

NANCE, CACCIATORE AND HAMILTON
525 North Harbor Blvd.
Melbourne, Florida 32935
Tel: 321.254.8416

GERRARO & ASSOCIATES, P.A.
First Union Financial Center
200 South Biscayne Bouldvard, Suite 3800
Miami, Florida 33131
Tel: 305.375.0111

Cantor, Arkema and Edmonds, P.C.
First National Bank Building
823 East Main Street
P.O. Box 561

Richmond, VA 32318-0561
Tel: 804.644.1400

Thomasson, Gilbert, Cook & Maguire, LC
715 North Clark
P.O. Box 1180
Cape Girardeau, Missouri 63702-1180
Tel: 573.335.6651

WALLACE & GRAHAM
525 N. Main Street
Salisbury, North Carolina 28144
Tel: 704-633-5244

THE HENDLER LAW FIRM, P.C.
816 Congress Avenue, Suite 1100
Austin, Texas 78701
Tel: 512.473.3672

I have written numerous letters to the press about the Thimerosal (mercury)

That is in baby vaccines and have yet to receive any type of response.

It was my hope that the press would look into this matter. I know articles have been written and the public is aware of this problem. My question to the press is....
Do they know the full story? Are they willing to report on all aspects of this tragedy?

Below is a letter I wrote to all of the television networks. It spells out the causes and the whole issue of mercury poisoning. I even included a Material Safety Data Sheet (MSDS) on Thimerosal. The MSDS is an un bias report on what thimerosal actually is and what it does to the human brain.

The MSDS on Thimerosal will set the record straight, once and for all. It is interesting to note that the press is very reluctant to print the MSDS in the major publications. Does this sound familiar?

I pleaded with these news people to make the MSDS main stream public knowledge.....

No Response........WHY?

12/15/2002 ATTN: NEWS DESK

TO: NBC NEWS, CBS, ABC, CNN, FOX, A/P News / New York

Re: Autism-Mercury Poisoning-Thimerosal Link

Attn: News Anchor

Dear Sirs

I have been watching your news broadcasts for along time and feel compelled to write you this letter.

We have a six year old boy named Ian. He was born perfectly normal with no complications at birth. During his first year of life, Ian was an active, playful baby who showed no signs of being developmentally disabled. His pediatrician said Ian was absolutely perfect.

Ian, like most other children completed his baby vaccines on schedule.

After the first 16 months, Ian began to show signs of extreme stress and began crying all of the time. We took him to the doctors and they were concerned. Over the next three months, Ian slipped away and was eventually diagnosed with Autism.

The next year was terrible, Ian got worse and we were devastated. We watched our little boy go into oblivion. In

late 2000, we realized that there was something more that may have happened to Ian. Upon examination of his baby vaccines, we discovered by cross reference that our little boy received 17 injections and 13 of these injections contained the
additive called Thimerosal.

Thimerosal contains 49.6% mercury. Mercury is extremely neuro toxic and the damage is permanent. After exhaustive investigations and medical testing, we confirmed that our little boy was indeed mercury poisoned by the vaccines.

According to his weight, our boy received over 40 times the level of mercury that is considered safe by the E.P.A. from these vaccine injections.

We have since learned that there has been a 700 % increase in "Autism".

This is an alarming development. The families that have been devastated deserve answers.

Thimerosal was removed from pet vaccines 10 years ago because of the risk of mercury poisoning to animals. It is unbelievable why they would deliberately keep this stuff in baby vaccines. The pharmaceutical company's weighed their profits against the possibility of brain damage to our children. These children and their parents lost.

Today there are at least 6 class action law suits against the pharmaceutical company's who manufactured and sold these vaccines and probably hundreds of other suits pending.

Last month the Bush administration put in a last minute provision in the Homeland Security Bill that makes it more difficult to take the pharmaceutical company's to court.

The administration also is asking to "seal" CDC documents that show the dangers of thimerosal to children. The Bush administration knew the dangers and is trying to protect these company's. This is because President Bush's top advisory staff are current and former Eli Lilly executives and that President Bush's father sat on the board of Eli Lilly Co. for a number of years and former Vice President Quayle's family controls Lilly Co.

Is this corruption at the highest level of government? Does this violate the 7th and 14th Constitutional Amendments of the U.S.? Does this violate the very spirit of the Freedom of Information Act?

Why is the administration further damaging the lives of these children by not allowing legal due process in a court of law? Sadly, this is all corruption at the top executive level of our government. What happened to "With Liberty and Justice for All"? I guess this only applies to the rich and of course the powerful people in our government. What about these little, innocent children who have been permanently brain damaged?

The U.S. government obviously does not represent these people and is obviously supporting the pharmaceutical industry that in fact poisoned these children simply for increased corporate profits. Are political payoffs and donations by the pharmaceutical company's to the GOP more important then these children's brains? The executive branch of our government obviously thinks it is!

The current argument in the media is…..**does thimerosal cause autism**?

The pharmaceutical company's have put a cleaver spin on this to direct the press to ask this mis-guided question. By their design, the pharmaceutical company's know that there are no real answers to this question because autism is very difficult to quantify in legal and medical terms at this time. This is an argument that the pharmaceutical industry knows that they will win every time. They have been successful at this manipulation.

The press needs to be told the truth regarding thimerosal. About what it does and more importantly, about the tragic damage it has already done to thousands of children.

It is very interesting to note some recent tests that were performed (that received press coverage) tried to disprove the link between "autism" and the vaccines.

The most recent test involved 33 children. The results were quoted as "no mercury was found in the blood samples!" This test was flawed in three ways.

1) Small sample size.
2) Thimerosal was not contained in the injections these children received.

3) Mercury absorbs in the tissues, not in the blood. Every physician knows this fact.

The vaccine manufactures finally removed this poison in 1999. However, the tragic damage had already been done. Many of these children that were poisoned before 1999 (when the thimerosal was in the vaccines) are receiving Chelation treatments that remove heavy metal from their tissues. The results of stool samples taken are horrifying.

The test results initiated after the chelation challenge protocols on these children are never reported on by the press. Why?

I think it would be in everyone's best interest to enlighten the public about what Thimerosal actually is and what it does to brain tissue.

I have enclosed the UN bias report on the chemical called Thimerosal. Please read this report and bring this to the public's attention. This report was completed by the chemical industry. Again, it is un bias and is required for industrial hazmat protocols.

Sirs,

I think it is very important that the truth be told. **These children are not Autistic, they are Mercury Poisoned.** This legal distinction between autism and mercury poisoning must be made. Mercury poisoning can be legally and medically measured and qualified in court. This issue will prevail in court. The GOP and the pharmaceutical company's know this simple truth. This is precisely why the Bush administration put the provision in the Homeland Security Bill that illegally protects this industry. These children deserve justice. Our government is NOT protecting these innocent children's rights.

Why isn't Ashcroft involved? Is it because he was the one who submitted the request to "seal" the CDC documentation? This whole issue between the Administrations protection of the pharmaceutical industry from legal litigation in the name of National Security is absolute corruption. How can mercury in baby vaccines be a matter of National Security? This is not National Security, it is FINANCIAL SECURITY for President Bush's friends in the pharmaceutical industry. Nothing more and nothing less!

These children's rights cannot be taken away by the politicians who are being manipulated and bought off by the pharmaceutical industry, which is responsible for this disaster.

The publics trust has been violated and a terrible tragedy has occurred. These children's lives were stolen and their parents' dreams were shattered.

I wonder if Dick Armey (R.Texas) is still proud of what he did? If so, then may God have mercy on this man's soul.

One last question, how much in campaign contributions did Senator Frist (R.Tenn) receive from the pharmaceutical industry? I understand he authored this illegal provision in the Homeland Security bill. This is an outrage and is simply unbelievable!

I commend Congressman Burton (R. Indiana) for his work so far. This man knows the truth and is trying to help these children get the help they need.

Dear Sirs,

I am not anti vaccines, they have prevented diseases. However, I am against an industry that intentionally put mercury in their products that did permanent brain damage to perfectly healthy children simply for increased corporate profits. This was wrong and with Gods help and **yours**, these deserving little children will get their day in court.

Respectfully Yours,

Courtney L. Zietzke
Father of Ian Zietzke

P.S.

A copy of the Material Safety Data Sheet (MSDS) is attached.
Please make this Public knowledge.

PUBLIC DOMAIN DOCUMENT

MSDS Name: Thimerosal

Catalog Numbers:
BP254210, BP2542100, BP254225, BP2542250, BP2542500
Synonyms:
Thimerosal; Merthiolate Sodium; Ethyl (2-Mercaptobenzoato-S) mercury
Sodium Salt; Sodium Ethylmercuric Thiosalicylate.,
Company Identification: Fisher Scientific

                     1 Reagent Lane
                     Fairlawn, NJ 07410

For information call: 201 – 796 – 7100
Emergency Number: 201 – 796 – 7100
For CHEMTREC assistance, call: 800 – 424 – 9300
For International CHEMTREC assistance, call: 703 – 527 – 3887

**** *SECTION 2 — COMPOSITION, INFORMATION ON INGEDIENTS* ****

CAS#	Chemical Name	%	EINECS#
54 – 64 8	Sodiumm o- (ethylmercurithio) benzoate	ca 100	200-210-4

Hazard Symbols: T
Risk Phrases: 25 33 36/37/38

**** *SECTION 3 — HAZARDS IDENTIFICATION* ****

EMERGENCY OVERVIEW

Appearance: white to white cream.

Warning! Causes respiratory tract irritation. May cause digestive tract irritation. Irritant. Toxic. Light sensitive. Harmful if swallowed. May cause central nervous system effects. May cause adverse reproductive effects based upon animal studies. Causes eye and skin irritation. Danger of cumulative effects.
Target Organs: Kidneys, central nervous system, spleen, bone.

Potential Health Effects

Eye:
Causes eye irritation. May cause chemical conjunctivitis.
Skin:
> Causes skin irritation. May cause skin sensitization, an allergic reaction, which becomes evident upon re-exposure to this material. May cause erythema (redness) and edema (fluid buildup) with crusting and scaling.

Ingestion:
> Harmful if swallowed. May cause gastrointestinal irritation with nausea, vomiting and diarrhea. May cause kidney damage. Mercaptans may cause nausea and headache. Exposure to high concentrations of mercaptans can produce unconsciousness with cyanosis (bluish discoloration of skin due to deficient oxygenation

of the blood), cold extremities and rapid pulse. May cause central nervous system effects and/or neurological effects. Human fatalities have been reported from acute poisoning.

Inhalation:

Causes respiratory tract irritation. May cause kidney damage. May cause allergic respiratory tract irritation. Exposure to high concentrations of mercaptans can produce unconsciousness with cyanosis (bluish discoloration of skin due to deficient oxygenation of the blood), cold extremities and rapid pulse. Mercaptans may cause nausea and headache. Can produce delayed pulmonary edema. Acute exposure to high concentrations of mercury vapors may cause severe respiratory tract irritation. May cause central, peripheral, and autonomic nervous system effects.

Chronic:

Effects may be delayed. Chronic exposure to mercury may cause permanent central nervous system damage, fatigue, weight loss, tremors, personality changes. Chronic ingestion may cause accumulation of mercury in body tissues. Chronic ingestion may result in salicylism which is characterized by nausea, vomiting, gastrointestinal ulcers, and hemorrhagic strokes. Adverse reproductive effects have been reported in animals. Chronic exposure to mercury vapors may produce weakness, fatigue, anorexia, loss of weight and gastrointestinal disturbances which is collectively referred to as asthenic-vegetative syndrome or micromercurialism. Chronic exposure to mercury compounds may produce immunologic glomerular disease.

**** *SECTION 4 — FIRST AID MEASURES* ****

Eyes:

Immediately flush eyes with plenty of water for at least 15 minutes, occasionally lifting the upper and lower eyelids. Get medical aid.

Skin:

Get medical aid. Flush skin with plenty of soap and water for at least 15 minutes while removing contaminated clothing and shoes. Wash clothing before reuse.

Ingestion:

Never give anything by mouth to an unconscious person. Get medical aid. Do NOT induce vomiting. If conscious and alert, rinse mouth and drink 2-4 cupfuls of milk or water.

Inhalation:

Remove from exposure to fresh air immediately. If not breathing, give artificial respiration. If breathing is difficult, give oxygen. Get medical aid. Do NOT use mouth-to-mouth resuscitation.

Notes to Physician:

Treat symptomatically and supportively. The concentration of mercury in whole blood is a reasonable measure of the body-burden of mercury and thus is used for monitoring purposes.

**** *SECTION 5 — FIRE FIGHTING MEASURES* ****

General Information:

As in any fire, wear a self-contained breathing apparatus in pressure-demand, MSHA/NIOSH (approved or equivalent), and full protective gear. During a fire, irritating and highly toxic gases may be generated by thermal decomposition or combustion. Use water spray to keep fire-exposed containers cool. Containers may explode when heated. Non-combustible, substance itself does not burn but may decompose upon heating to produce irritating, corrosive and/or toxic fumes.

Extinguishing Media:

Do NOT get water inside containers. For small fires, use dry chemical, carbon dioxide, or water spray. For large fires, use water spray, fog or regular foam. Cool containers with flooding quantities of water until well after fire is out.

Autoignition Temperature: Not available.

Flash Point: Not available

Explosion Limits, lower: Not available.

Explosion Limits, upper: Not available.

NFPA Rating: (estimated) Health: 2; Flammability: 0; Reactivity: 0

**** *SECTION 6 — ACCIDENTAL RELEASE MEASURES* ****

General Information: Use proper personal protective equipment as indicated in Section 8.

Spills/Leaks:

Avoid runoff into storm sewers and ditches which lead to waterways. Clean up spills immediately, observing precautions in the Protective Equipment section. Sweep up, then place into a suitable container for disposal. Avoid generating dusty conditions. Remove all sources of ignition. Provide ventilation.

**** *SECTION 7 — HANDLING and STORAGE* ****

Handling:

Minimize dust generation and accumulation. Avoid breathing dust, vapor, mist, or gas. Avoid contact with eyes, skin, and clothing. Keep container tightly closed. Avoid ingestion and inhalation. Use with adequate ventilation. Store protected from light. Wash clothing before reuse.

Storage:

Store in a tightly closed container. Store in a cool, dry, well-ventilated area away from incompatible substances. Keep away from metals. Store protected from light.

**** SECTION 8 — EXPOSURE CONTROLS, PERSONAL PROTECTION ****

Engineering Controls:

Facilities storing or utilizing this material should be equipped with an eyewash facility and a safety shower. Use adequate ventilation to keep airborne concentrations low.

Exposure Limits

Chemical Name	ACGIH	NIOSH	OSHA – Final PELs
Sodium o-(ethylmerc urithio) benzoate	0.025 mg/m3 TWA (listed under ** no name **) .as Hg: skin – potential for cutaneous absorption (listed under ** no name **).	0.05 mg/m3 TWA (listed under ** no name **) .10 mg/m3 IDLH (listed under ** no name **).	1mg/10m3 (vapor) (listed under ** no name **).

OSHA Vacated PELs:

Sodium o- (ethylmercurithiho) benzoate:

vapor, as Hg: 0.05 mg/m3 TWA (listed under ** no name **) 0.03 mg/m3 STEL (listed under ** no name **) aryl and inorganic, as Hg: C 0.1 mg/m3 (listed under ** no name **)

Personal Protective Equipment

Eyes: Wear appropriate protective eyeglasses or chemical safety goggles as described by OSHA's eye and face protection regulations in 29 CFR 1910.133 or European Standard EN166.

Skin: Wear appropriate protective gloves to prevent skin exposure.

Clothing: Wear appropriate protective clothing to prevent skin exposure.

Respirators: Follow the OSHA respirator regulations found in 29CFR 1910.134 or European Standard EN 149. Always use a NIOSH or European Standard EN 149 approved respirator when necessary.

**** SECTION 9 — PHYSICAL AND CHEMICAL PROPERTIES ****

Physical State:	Crystalline powder
Appearance:	white to light cream
Odor:	characteristic odor
pH:	Not available.
Vapor Pressure:	Not available.
Vapor Density:	Not available.
Evaporation Rate:	Not available
Viscosity:	Not available.
Boiling Point:	Not available.
Freezing/Melting Point:	232-233C
Decomposition Temperature:	> 233 deg C
Solubility in water:	Soluble.
Specific Gravity/ Density:	
Molecular Formula:	C9H9HgNa02S
Molecular Weight:	404.82

**** *SECTION 10 — STABILITY AND REACTIVITY* ****

Chemical Stability:

> Stable at room temperature in closed containers under normal storage and handling conditions.

Conditions to Avoid:

> Incompatible materials, light, dust generation, excess heat, strong oxidants.

Incompatibilities with Other Materials:

> Strong acids, strong bases, strong oxidizing agents.

Hazardous Decomposition Products:

> Carbon monoxide, oxides of sulfur, carbon dioxide, hydrogen sulfide, mercury/mercury oxides, sodium oxide.

Hazardous Polymerization: Has not been reported.

**** *SECTION 11 — TOXICOLOGICAL INFORMATION* ****

RTECS#:

CAS# 54-64-8: OV8400000

LD50/LC50:

CAS# 54-64-8: Draize test, rabbit, eye: 8 ug Mild; Oral, mouse: LD50 = 91 mg/kg; Oral, rat: LD50 = 75 mg/kg

Carcinogenicity:

Sodium o- (ethylmercurithio) benzoate – ACGIH: A4 – Not Classifiable as a Human Carcinogen (listed as ** IARC: Group 3 carcinogen (listed as ** undefined **).

Epidemiooogy:

Experimental reproductive, and teratogenic effects have been reported.

Teratogenicity:

Teratogenic effects have occurred in experimental animals.

Reproductive Effects:

Reproductive effects have occurred in experimental animals.

Neurotoxicity:

No information available.

Mutagaenicity:

Mutagenic effects have occurred in experimental animals.

Other Studies:

The hazards associated with mercury compounds may be seen in this product. See actual entry in RTECS for complete information.

**** *SECTION 12 — ECOLOGICAL INFORMATION* ****

**** *SECTION 13 — DISPOSAL CONSIDERATIONS* ****

Chemical waste generators must determine whether a discarded chemical is classified as a hazardous waste.

US EPA guidelines for the classification determination are listed in 40 CFR Parts 261.3. Additionally, waste generators must consult state and local hazardous waste regulations to ensure complete and accurate classification.

RCRA P-Series: None listed.

RCRA U-Series: None listed.

**** *SECTION 14 — TRANSPORT INFORMATION* ****

US DOT

Shipping Name: **SMALL QTY EXCEPTION SEE 48 CFR 173.4**

Canadian TDG

No information available.

****** SECTION 15 — REGULATORY INFORMATION ******

US FEDERAL

TSCA

CAS# 54-64-8 is listed on the TSCA inventory.

Health & Safety Reporting List

None of the chemicals are on the Health & Safety Reporting List.

Chemical Test Rules

None of the chemicals in this product are under a Chemical Test Rule.

Section 12b

None of the chemicals are listed under TSCA Section 12b.

TSCA Significant New Use Rule

None of the chemicals in this material have a SNUR under TSCA.

SARA

Section 302 (RQ)

None of the chemicals in this material have an RQ.

Section 302 (TPQ)

None of the chemicals in this product have a TPQ.

SARA Codes

CAS # 54-64-8: acute, chronic.

Section 313

> This chemical is not at a high enough concentration to be reportable under Section 313.

Clean Air Act:

CAS# 54-64-8 listed as ** no name ** is listed as a hazardous air pollutant (HAP).

This material does not contain any Class 1 Ozone depletors.

This material does not contain any Class 2 Ozone depletors.

Clean Water Act:

> None of the chemicals in this product are listed as Hazardous Substances under the CWA.

> CAS# 54-64-8 is listed as a Priority Pollutant under the Clean Water Act.

> CAS# 54-64-8 is listed as a Toxic Pollutant under the Clean Water Act.

OSHA:

None of the chemicals in this product are considered highly hazardous by OSHA.

STATE

> Sodium o- (ethylmercurithio) ben can be found on the following state right to know lists: California, (listed as ** no name **), California, (listed as ** no name **), New Jersey, (listed as ** no name **), Florida, (listed as ** no name **), Pennsylvania, (listed as ** no name **), Pennsylvania, (listed as ** no name **), Minnesota,

(listed as ** no name **), Massachusetts, (listed as ** no name **).

WARNING: This product contains Sodium o-(ethylmercurithio) benzoate, listed as ' ** undefined **', a chemical known to the state of California to cause birth defects or other reproductive harm.

California No Significant Risk Level:

None of the chemicals in this product are listed.

European/International Regulations

European Labeling in Accordance with EC Directives

Hazard Symbols: T

Risk Phrases:

R 25 Toxic if swallowed.

R 33 Danger of cumulative effects.

R 36/37/38 Irritating to eyes, respiratory system and skin.

Safety Phrases:

S 2 Keep out of reach of children.

S 13 Keep away from food, drink and animal feeding stuffs.

S 28A After contact with skin, wash immediately with plenty of water.

S 36 Wear suitable protective clothing.

S 45 In case of accident of if you feel unwell, seek medical advice immediately (show the label where possible).

WGK (Water Danger/Protection)

CAS# 53-64-8: 3

United Kingdom Occupational Exposure Limits

CAS# 54-64-8: OES-United Kingdom, TWA (listed as ** undefined **): as Hg: 0.025 mg/m3 TWA; (does not include mercury alkyls)

Canada

CAS# 54-64-8 is listed on Canada's DSL List.

This product has a WHMIS classification on D1B, D2A, D2B.

CAS# 54-64-8 is listed on Canada's Ingredient Disclosure List.

Exposure Limits

CAS# 54-64-8: OEL-AUSTRALIA:TWA 0.05 mg(Hg) /m3;Skin JANUARY 1993

OEL-BELGIUM:TWA 0.05 mg(Hg) /m3;Skin JANUARY 1993

OEL-CZECHOSLOVAKIA:TWA 0.05 mg(Hg) / m3;STEL 0.15 mg(Hg) /m3

OEL-DENMARK:TWA 0.05 mg(Hg) /m3 JANUARY 1993

OEL-FINLAND:TWA 0.05 mg(Hg) /3 JANUARY 1993

Courtney L. Zietzke

OEL-FRANCE:TWA 0.05 mg(Hg) /m3 JANUARY 1993

OEL-GERMANY:TWA 0.01 ppm (o.1 mg(Hg) /m3) JANUARY 1993

OEL-HUNGARY:TWA 0.02 mg(Hg) /m3;STEL 0.04 mg(Hg) /m JANUARY 1993

OEL-JAPAN:TWA 0.05 mg(Hg) /m3 JANUARY 1993

OEL-THE NETHERLANDS:TWA 0.05 mg(Hg) / m3;STEL 0.15 mg(Hg) /m3

OEL-THE PHILIPPINES:TWA 0.05 mg(Hg) /m3 JANUARY 1993

OEL-POLAND:TWA 0.01 mg(Hg) /m3 JANUARY 1993

OEL-RUSSIA:TWA 0.05 mg(Hg) /m3;STEL 0.01 mg(Hg) /m3 JANUARY 1993

OEL-SWEDEN:TWA 0.05 mg(Hg) /m3 JANUARY 1993

OEL-THAILAND:STEL 0.05 mg(Hg) /m3 JANUARY 1993

OEL-UNITED KINGDOM:TWA 0.05 mg(Hg) / m3;STEL 0.15 mg(Hg) /m3

OEL IN BULGARIA, COLOMBIA, JORDAN, KOREA check ACGIH TLV

OEL IN NEW ZEALAND, SINGAPORE, VIETNAM check ACGI TLV

OEL-AUSTRALIA:TWA 0.05 mg(Hg) /m3;Skin JANUARY 1993

OEL-BELGIUM:TWA   0.05   mg(Hg)   /m3;Skin
JANUARY 1993

OEL-CZECHOSLOVAKIA:TWA   0.05   mg(Hg)   /
m3;STEL 0.15 mg(Hg) /m3

OEL-DENMARK:TWA 0.05 mg(Hg) /m3 JANUARY
1993

OEL-FINLAND:TWA 0.05 mg(Hg) /m3 JANUARY

**** *SECTION 16 — ADDITIONAL INFORMATION* ****

MSDS Creation Date: 2/02/2000 Revision #2 Date: 8/02/2000

The information above is believed to be accurate and represents the best information currently available to us. However, we make no warranty of merchantability or any other warranty, express or implied, with respect to such information, and we assume no liability resulting from its use. Users should make their own investigations to determine the suitability of the information for their particular purposes. In no way shall the company be liable for any claims, losses, or damages of any third party or for lost profits or any special, indirect, incidental, consequential or exemplary damages, howsoever arising, even if the company has been advised of the possibility of such damages.

The most damaging evidence against the Pharmaceutical Industry and their Governmental protectors is in the following text.

This letter was addressed to Congressman, Dan Burton (R. Indiana)
This is interesting, because Indiana is where the drug giant Eli Lilly is located.

I guess blood is thicker then money after all…All it takes is one good and honest Congressman and his vaccine / mercury poisoned grandchild to bring more of this tragedy to light.

This letter clearly states what has happened and that the Governmental officials at the CDC and the FDA blatantly, absolutely, 100%, LIED!

After I read the following article, I began to re-think the three year Statute of Limitation law regarding the Vaccine Court.(pharmaceutical controlled)

The next time this so-called American Hall of "Justice" dismisses a case because of the three year rule, the "corporate" judge in this court should be held in contempt of a higher court, The Supreme Court. This court is clearly UN-Constitutional, how can it not be?

The Vaccine Injury court denies equal protection under the law and it is prejudice.

Please read the following article………….Important!!

[This letter was sent to Congressman Burton from Liz Birt. Liz is Counsel for Safe Minds, the founder of Medical Interventions for Autism, and a parent of a child with autism. Liz was responsible for obtaining the "secret" CDC VSD Study and the Simpsonwood meeting minutes for Safe Minds though the Freedom of Information Act.]

March 7, 2002   **Public Domain**

Congressman Dan Burton

Chairman Exhibit # 6

Government Reform Committee

United States House of Representatives

2157 Rayburn House Office Building

Washington, D.C.

Re: British Medical Journal Article, May 27, 1972 "Danger of Skin Burns

>From Thiomersal"; Adverse Drug Reactions Acute Poisoning Revenue

Article, 1986 "Organic mercury compounds and their toxicity" ("1986 Adverse Drug Reaction Article") Testimony by Dr. William Egan, FDA and Dr. Roger Bernier, CDC on July 18, 2000

Dear Congressman Burton:

As you requested I am sending to you copies of the above referenced articles. As you can see, much was known about thimerosal prior to 1999. I am sure that through the process of subpoenas we will discover much more.

Of particular note is the 1986 Adverse Drug Reaction Article written by K.A. Winship, Senior Medical Officer, Medicines Division, Department of Health and Social Security for the United Kingdom. It is my understanding that this pierson would be in a similar position as a top administrative officer of our FDA. Page 171 of this article states: "Multidose vaccines and allergy-testing extracts contain a cercurial preservative, usually 0.01% thiomersal, and may present problems occasionally in practice. It is therefore, now accepted that multidose injection preparations are undesirable and that preservatives should not be present in unit-dose preparations (emphasis added)."

On July 18, 2000 you asked Dr. William Egan of the FDA the following question: When did the FDA and CDC first start being concerned about mercury in vaccines?" Dr. Egan responded, "I guess the major concern started somewhere around May of 1999?" I can not believe based upon articles such as this that the FDA did not know that thimerosal was a problem in vaccines before may of 1999. If a senior official in the United Kingdom stated as a matter of fact in 1986 that multidose preparations were undesirable because of thimerosal what were our FDA officials doing? My "hunch" is that there was extreme pressure from the drug companies not to make a change because of cost. Here we are 15 years later and the FDA has not mandated that thimerosal be removed from all vaccines nor has it acted to recall pediatric vaccines containing thimerosal. I find the conduct of our FDA officials reprehensible.

In addition, Dr. Egan at the same July 18, 2000 hearing was asked the following question by Congresswoman Chenowith-Hage "With regards to the introduction of the HIB vaccine and hepatitis B vaccine, could you advise the committee on what studies were done with regards to these new vaccines that would prove thimerosal was safe?" Dr. Egan's response was "There was a long history of the use, the safe use of thiomerosal, you know, in vaccines since they were- since it was first introduced. And at that time (1990) there was no data to suggest that the added mercury from the introduction of those new vaccines would be harmful." Congressman Burton, I find this statement by Dr. Egan to be patently false. By 1990 there was a mountain of evidence that thimerosal was unsafe and ineffective. In point of fact, in 1987 the Commission of the European Communities initiated a research project of 10 known or suspected spindle poisons including thimerosal. In 1993, as described in Mutuation Research, 287 (1993) 17-22 thimerosal was identified as a strong inhibitor of microtubular assembly, a process which is essential for proper neuronal development. Again, I find it incomprehensible that officials at our FDA could have overlooked this research, if they did so they are grossly incompetent. In addition, since 1992 the FDA has employed a researcher by the name of Joan May to test thimerosal in various biologic products including vaccines. If the use of thimerosal was proven to be safe why was the person employed by FDA?

In addition, I would also like to point out testimony given by Dr. Roger Bernier of the CDC at the July 18, 2000 hearing that was false. Dr. Bernier was questioned by Congressman Waxman as follows: Congressman Waxman: "The question that I would like to ask, and I am sure parents want to know, is this being done because there are known adverse related events or as a precautionary measure? CDC convened an expert panel to examine data that showed a possible weak link between thimerosal and certain developmental delays. The panel presented its findings to CDC's Advisory Committee on Immunization Practices and concluded that the data were insufficient to show a causal connection between thimerosal and certain developmental delays. Is that true? Is that the position that the CDC has taken?" Dr. Bernier responded: "That's correct, Mr. Waxman. At the present time CDC has no evidence of harm to any children from thimerosal in vaccines. We have constantly acted to look at safety. Following the episode last summer, CDC did begin to look at the data in the Vaccine Safety Datalink, and one of the outcomes was autism, and there was no suggestion of any association between thimerosal exposure and autism in the Vaccine Safety Datalink study.(emphasis added)"

Congressman Burton, based upon the documents that CDC turned over to SAFEMINDs last year I believe that Dr. Bernier perjured himself at the July 18, 2000 hearing. My belief is based upon the following facts: 1) Dr. Verstraeten's 2/29/00 VSD study found a relative risk for autism of 2.48 at a thimerosal exposure of 62.5 mcgs of thimerosal and above; 2) Dr. Verstraeten's 2/29/00 and 6/1/00 VSD studies found a statistically significant positive correlation between: 1) the cumulative exposure at 2 months of age and unspecified developmental delay; 2) the cumulative exposure at 3 months of age and tics; 3) the cumulative exposure at 6 months of age and attention deficit disorder; 4) the cumulative exposure at 1, 3 and 6 months of age and language and speech delays; and 5) the cumulative exposure at 1, 3 and 6 months of age and neurodevelopmental delays in general. Dr. Bernier was copied on both of these studies. I do not believe he was truthful in his testimony when he made these categorical remarks to your committee.

As you can probably tell from my comments I am extremely distrustful of individuals at CDC and FDA. They have a history of outright lying. In addition, when possible they engage in the distortion of facts to suit their purposes. Please know that I am committed to finding out the truth about the relationship of vaccines to neurodevelopmental disorders including autism. I am willing to work on any project that would be useful to your committee at any time without compensation. I feel that this work must be done for the children and their families.

Thank you for your support on this matter.

Best Regards,

Liz Birt

What I have tried to do in this short but specific work was to present the facts and the truth, the whole truth and nothing but the truth, I think you know the rest of that phrase. The question is, does the government?

Why are they afraid of exposure in these cases? Why have they taken extraordinary steps to prevent anyone of these children's legal cases from ever going to trial?

Why have they LIED? Why did the Bush Administration try to seal CDC documents that clearly show the danger of thimerosal to children?

Why did the Bush administration put a last minute provision in the Homeland Security Bill to thwart any legal action on behalf of the thousands of mercury poisoned, neurologically damaged children? Why did they try to hide additional information?

These are questions that need honest, straight forward answers. As of yet, absolutely no credible answers or information has been given. Instead, the parents of these brain damaged children have been given the run around and the usual denial of the truth.

I am not the most intelligent person out there; however, I do know that government officials upon taking office are required to take the OATH of office. This oath requires these people to uphold and defend the constitution of the United States of America.

Did these government people that are involved in this obvious cover up defend the rights of these children as provided for them in the Constitution?

Does the government vaccine court provide impartiality? Is it fair?

The most innocent victims of all time have been lead to the slaughter.

These children and their parents never had a choice in any of this tragedy. The thimerosal laden vaccines that these children received were mandated by the U.S. government as necessary. Parents were informed that their children were required to have all of their vaccines or they would not be permitted to attend public schools. This was like shooting fish in a barrel.

In the case of the tobacco settlements, people had a choice weather or not to smoke.
The tobacco industry warned people for years that smoking was hazardous to their health.

The vaccine industry never warned, never disclosed and then paid the government via their generous donations and stock options to help them cover this up. In fact, they even created their own private UNCONSTITUTIONAL, three year statute court of law, the vaccine court, where no injured child could ever possibly win a case. This was by design, it was calculating and it was criminal.

I, as an American citizen believe in this country, its principles and its legal system.

President Bush (Sr.) also believes in this country, when he was president, he insisted that the Congress pledge allegiance to the flag..........remember that?

Well, what does the pledge of allegiance say? The last six words are the most important.

I pray that people try to understand the magnitude of what has happened to these children. Their lives were stolen and their parents' dreams were shattered, all because of corporate greed. The financial hardship these parents have had to endure is terrible, they will probably never recover financially or emotionally. Justice must be served. This is America not some backward civilization from the dark ages.

This true and tragic story had to be told. These children and their parents were victimized. All that is needed is an impartial jury to look at the facts and decide what's fair and to decide the legal outcome of these crimes against these children and their parents.

This is clearly what the Pharmaceutical industry and the Government DOES NOT want.

These people know they will loose in court. They will smoke screen this, they will deny liability, and finally they will quote the usual National Security bullshit. Then, after all else, they will try to get jurisdiction into their own private pharmaceutical court. This is wrong and this is an outrage.

We are Americans, we pay taxes and we should not let these people take away our Constitutional rights and further damage our children.

If I am sued as a result of this book, then maybe I'll be lucky and be taken to the Vaccine Court, where I will get a free pass, a governmental cover up, A, "I don't recall" or a three year statute of limitations rule from public officials.

I can also take the fifth, but I have no intention of doing that. I did not commit the crime, the government and the pharmaceutical industry did. I will not suppress, conceal or distort any information as they clearly have done.

On Feb 20, 2003 the President was forced to sign the "official" repeal order that will remove the special interest provisions from the Homeland Security Act. Great News!

It is interesting to note that when the repealed sections were finely signed, this was not in any of the major newspapers. Does this sound familiar? This was finely something to smile about.....Fair and equal justice could finely start to be administered. Why didn't the press report on this event? This was a small victory for these parents and their vaccine injured children.

However, Senate Majority leader Bill Frist (R. Tenn) has introduced new and sweeping legislation that **again** protects the pharmaceutical industry from liability in thimerosal – mercury class action law suits. Title II of this bill STINKS! It will go to the Senate floor in mid to late 2004 all in the name of the old favorite.......National Security!.... Unbelievable! How can mercury in child vaccines be a matter of national security? This is not national security; this is financial security for the drug companies. This is pure criminal, nothing more and nothing less.

I have enclosed a copy of this document at the end of this book. This document is an atrocity. This is incredible, check this out. You won't believe this crap came from our in "God We Trust" Government. While reading this garbage it will become clearly obvious to the reader that the pharmaceutical lawyers wrote this Bill. Can Mr. Frist and his pharmaceutical legal "friends" spell the word UNCONSTITUTIONAL? This bill CANNOT be signed into law. Call your Senators and call your Representatives and tell these people... NO!

It should be noted that Mr. Frist is in fact a prominent medical doctor who has extensive political and financial ties to the pharmaceutical industry. He was the original author of the Lilly provision that protected the drug industry. When congress voted down the provision, the white house just turned around and sneaked it in at the last minute in the Homeland Security Bill.....More criminal behavior, courtesy of the Executive Branch of our U.S. Government. A law suit protection provision for the pharmaceutical companies is not a matter of National Security in any way, shape or form. You can't even compare or rationalize this argument. The American people are not stupid.

This vaccine bill violates the Constitution of the United States of America.

Remember, WE THE PEOPLE? The pharmaceutical industry CANNOT be protected at the expense of thousands of mercury poisoned children. They committed a crime and now this industry must pay for its mistakes and the subsequent cover ups.

Is money that important? To these people it sure is. Remember share holder value?

The executive branch of our government is trying to further damage these children by denying monetary assistance needed by families in order to properly care for these mercury poisoned children. This is further evidence of political corruption at its worst.

In the following pages are numerous public articles that finely begin detail this whole mess and put this puzzle together.

What I have endeavored to do in this book is to put all of this information together That paints the obvious picture.

The truth must be told, justice must be served and individual liberties and freedom cannot be taken away. This is the founding principle of this country's independence and the U.S. Constitution. This guiding principle cannot be bought or compromised by any politician, special interest, corporate group and or any subversive agency within our society.

Every honest person I have ever talked with regarding this tragedy has said, "How could these people ever commit these horrible injustices against these innocent children?

And continue doing so?" Well, they did and will continue to do so until they are stopped.

God himself who will be the ultimate judge regarding these peoples actions. Simple truth and common human decency will prevail.
I pray for these children, their parents and for this country……

**THE UNITED STATES OF AMERICA……….IN GOD
WE *STILL* TRUST!**

Exhibit # 1

Public Domain

Bush Admin. Withdraws Motion to Seal Thimerosal Documents in Current Cases

WASHINGTON, Dec. 19 /PRNewswire/ —

WASHINGTON, Dec. 19 /PRNewswire/ — The US Department of Justice agreed today to withdraw its motion to the US Court of Federal Claims Office of Special Master to seal all documents related to present thimerosal-autism claims. The Mercury Policy Project and SAFE MINDs said that the withdrawal of the motion was a step in the right direction. However, the groups questioned whether documents in future cases would be subject to the secrecy order.

"The Bush Administration has overreached in its attempt to seal documents in thimerosal cases and the withdrawal of their motion bears that out," said Michael Bender, director of the Mercury Policy Project. "Unfortunately, this agreement only addresses half the loaf of bread. While the motion's withdrawal may help those involved in current litigation, it leaves unresolved what this means for future cases."

While the groups acknowledge that some information unearthed in court should be kept private – like trade secrets – they maintain that scientific studies and information should not quality. In addition to the documents obtained through discovery from Eli Lilly, these also include unreleased confidential documents from the Centers for Disease Control stating that mercury in children's vaccines is a potential source of neurological damage in children including ADD/ADHD, speech and language delays and other neurological disorders including autism.

"We question the Bush Administration's blatant attempt to hide from the American public documents affecting the health and safety of millions of children – especially when the material in question is as dangerous as mercury," said Lyn Redwood, Pres. SAFE MINDs. "What are they trying to hide?"

While federal law typically seals documents in individual cases, it has not been applied to omnibus proceedings like the autism cases.

"What's the policy argument for such incredible secrecy?" said Sallie Bernard, executive director of SAFE MINDs. "The timing and the scope of this unprecedented secrecy action by the Bush Administration raises serious questions, considering that lawmakers have pledged to revisit the thimerosal liability shield provision in the Homeland Security Act when they return in January."

"The Bush Administration's secrecy request was premature, highly unusual and went against federal rules that impose severe restrictions on sealing of documents," said MPP director Bender. "The public – and especially families of autistic children – have a right to know about what Eli Lilly knew and when they knew it, both now and into the future."

The Mercury Policy Project and SAFE MINDs are non-profit organizations dedicated to reducing and eliminating mercury exposure and improving children's health and environmental outcomes through the elimination, treatment, and scientific investigations of mercury, regardless of its source, including thimerosal in medical products.

More information is available at – http://www.safeminds.org

http://www.mercurypolicy.org

LEGAL NEWS: *Top Headlines • Supreme Court • Commentary • Crime • Cyberspace • International*

US FEDERAL LAW: *Constitution• Codes • Supreme Court Opinions • Circuit Opinions*

US STATE LAW: *State Constitutions • State Codes • Case Law*

RESEARCH: *Dictionary • Forms • LawCrawler • Library • Summaries of Law*

LEGAL SUBJECTS: *Constitutional • Intellectual Property • Criminal • Labor • more...*

GOVERNMENT RESOURCES: *US Federal • US State • Directories • more....*

INTERNATIONAL RESOURCES: *Country Guides • Trade • World Constitutions • more...*

COMMUNITY: *Message Boards • Newsletters • Greedy Associates Boards*

TOOLS: *Office • Calendar • Email • West WorkSpace • FirmSites*

Exhibit # 2

Thimerosal Content in Some U.S. Licensed Vaccines
updated 09-30-99

This information appears on the http://www.vaccinesafety.edu/cc-thim.htm

Vaccine	Brand Name	Manufacturer	Thimerosal Concentration[1]	Mercury ug/0.5 ml
DTaP	Acel-Imune	Lederle Laboratories	.01%	25
	Tripedia	Pasteur Merieux Connaught	.01%	25
	Certiva	North American Vaccine	.01%	25
	Infanrix	SmithKline Beecham	0	0
DTwP	All Products		.01%	25
DT	All Products		.01%	25
Td	All Products		.01%	25
TT	All Products		.01%	25
DTwP-Hib	Tetramune	Lederle Laboratories	.01%	25
Hib	ActHIB	Pasteur Merieux Connaught	0	0
	TriHIBit	Pasteur Merieux Connaught	.01%	25
	HibTITER (multi-dose)	Lederle Laboratories	.01%	25
	HibTITER (single dose)	Lederle Laboratories	0	0
	Omni HIB	SmithKline Beecham	0	0
	PedvaxHIB liquid[2]	Merck	0	0
	COMVAX[3]	Merck	0	0
	ProHIBit[4]	Pasteur Merieux Connaught	.01%	25
Hepatitis B	Engerix-B	SmithKline Beecham	.005%	12.5

	Recombivax HB	Merck	.005%	12.5
NEW	Recombivax HB preservative free	Merck	0	0
Hepatitis A	Havrix	SmithKline Beecham	0	0
	Vaqta	Merck	0	0
IPV	IPOL	Pasteur Merieux Connaught	0	0
OPV	Orimune	Lederle Laboratories	0	0
MMR	MMR-II	Merck	0	0
Varicella	Varivax	Merck	0	0
Rotavirus	Rotashield	Wyeth-Ayerst	0	0
Lyme	LYMErix	SmithKline Beecham	0	0
Influenza	All Products		.01%	25
Meningococcal	Menomune A, C, AC and A/C/Y/W-135	CLI	.01%	25
Pneumococcal	Pnu-Imune 23	Lederle Laboratories	.01%	25
	Pneumovax 23	Merck	0	0
Rabies	Rabies Vaccine Adsorbed	BioPort Corporation	.01%	25
	IMOVAX	Pasteur Merieux Connaught	0	0
	Rabavert	Chiron	0	0
Typhoid Fever	Typhim Vi	Pasteur Merieux Connaught	0	0
	Typhoid Ty21a	Vivotef Berna	0	0
	Typhoid vaccine	Wyeth-Ayerst	0	0
Yellow Fever	YF-Vax	Pasteur Merieux Connaught	0	0
Anthrax	Anthrax vaccine	BioPort Corporation	0	0

1. *A concentration of 1:10,000 is equivalent to a 0.01% concentration. Thimerosal is approximately 50% Hg by weight. A 1:10,000 concentration contains 25 micrograms of Hg per 0.5 mL.*

2. *A previously marketed lyophilized preparation contained .05% thimerosal.*

3. *COMVAX is not approved for use under 6 weeks of age because of decreased response to the Hib component.*

4.   *ProHIBit is recommended by the Academy only for children 12 months of age and older.*

Exhibit # 3

Public Domain

November 27, 2002

The Honorable John D. Ashcroft

Attorney General of the United States

U.S. Department of Justice

10th Street and "Constitution Avenue, N.W.

Washington, DC 20510

Dear Mr. Attorney General:

Today's edition of the New York Times reported that the U.S. Department of Justice has asked a federal claims court to seal documentes about the potential hazards of thimerosal, a mercury-based preservative in vaccines that some claim has caused autism and other neurological disorders in children ("Justice Dept. Seeks to Seal Vaccine Papers," November 27).

If the report is accurate, the U.S. government is seeking to deprive parents of critical information about this preservative, which was used in vaccines up until 2001. Consumers Union, the nonprofit publisher of Consumer Reports magazine, asks that the Justice Department's action be stopped immediately.

Vaccines protect millions of children from contracting debilitating and sometimes fatal diseases. But news reports about cases of catastrophic reactions to vaccines have raised concerns among some parents about vaccine safety. Openness and transparency are the beset response to parents' concerns. Sealing these documents would be an outrageous move that would not only deny families from seeing relevant information concerning their children, but it could also fan the fears of parents who might choose not to have their children immunized at all.

News of the Justice Department's action follows the actions of members of Congress who inserted a provision in the homeland security bill that was intended to protect Eli Lilly, the manufacturer of thimerosal, from lawsuits over the preservative. We are particularly concerned that Eli Lilly has exerted undue influence over the political process. Surely the Justice Department believes that the interests of sick children are more important than the interests of the drug industry.

Sincerely,

Sally J. Greenberg

Senior Product Safety Counsel

Consumers Union Washington DC Office

View Files Sorted By Office: *Sonsumers Union OPI, New York – Washington DC Office*

West Coast Regional Office – Southwest Regional Office – Consumer Policy Institute

Courtney L. Zietzke

Congressman questions officials at Thimerosal hearings

06/20-2002

By *VALERI WILLIAMS* / WFAA-TV, Dallas

Public Domain

Exhibit # 4

A United States congressman is calling for criminal penalties for any government agency that knew about the dangers of Thimerosal in vaccines, and did nothing to protect American children.

Last month, a News 8 Investigation disclosed allegations that some government officials may have suppressed documentation about the risks. Some of those officials testified at Wednesday's congressional hearing.

News 8 research showed that the FDA began asking questions about the dangers of Thimerosal back in 1972. By 1992, the preservative had been pulled out of dog vaccines and contact lens solutions because of the risks.

However, it remained in vaccines for children until last year.

Government health officials squirmed uncomfortably in their seats Wednesday as more evidence emerged suggesting that they misled the public.

"You mean to tell me that since 1929, we've been using Thimerosal," Congressman Dan Burton (R-Indiana) said to the officials, "and the only test that you know of is from 1929, and every one of those people had meningitis, and they all died?"

For nearly an hour, Burton repeatedly asked FDA and CDC officials what they knew and when they knew it. And when memories seemed to be a bit fuzzy, the congressman produced old memos as a refresher.

One memo, from 1999, states that the FDA had an "interim plan … already in place for many years" to get rid of Thimerosal.

The same e-mail also addresses the FDA's fear that it will be accused by the public of being "asleep at the switch for decades, by allowing a dangerous compound to remain in childhood vaccines".

Burton has proposed bringing criminal charges if it's proven the government agencies were involved in a cover-up.

"Look, I don't think it makes any difference whether it's a private company or a government agency," Burton said. "If they know they're harming somebody and they continue to let it happen, then they should be held accountable."

Government accountability is something that parents of autistic children have been asking for for years.

Cooper Earp, 7, had lost his ability to talk by age three, and his mercury levels were off the charts. His parents said Cooper's only exposure to mercury was through his vaccines.

Today, he has all the classic signs of autism, such as repeatedly hitting himself, and fixating on such things as a spinning chair.

Cooper's mother Kristi Earp has a dream that one day Cooper will call her "mommy" in a sentence.

"I probably have that dream once a week that he's speaking to me. It would be wonderful," Earp said.

Parents like Earp would like to ask the panel of government officials why, in eighty years, they never ordered one clinical test on the effects of Thimerosal in vaccines.

Burton asked the question several times Wednesday, but never got a direct answer.

After the hearing, News 8 asked the same question of an official, walking briskly down a corridor.

"You have to call the press office," an assistant replied.

Burton has a personal stake in the growing scandal: he said his grandson became autistic a few days after receiving nine inoculations.

Thus far, within the government, Burton has been a minority voice, but he has subpoena power, and he keeps threatening to use it.

"So what you do is keep making the case, and keep trying to get the message out to a broader and broader audience so that people start saying 'Why?'," Burton said. "When enough people say 'Why?', change starts to take place."

Fair Use Policy

Gazette *Front Page Alphabetical Index to Site Site Search Our Sponsor*

Department of Psychology

Back to Kohl's Newsletter Index

Public Domain

Exhibit # 5

More on the Thimerosal-laced Infant Vaccine Outrage

Friends,

I am sending the following E-mail in it's entirety to Senator Hatch, who just happens to be one of the senators from my state.

I just received a response from him today in reference to a letter I mailed to him about my grave concerns over the implementation of the Homeland Security Act, which he worked very hard on getting passed.

He defended his work on this, and went on to explain all the benefits we'd realize... Well, I think I'm going to challenge him to sniff out the rat who added this Lilly white protection money to the Act...

PROTECTION MONEY

The Health Sciences Institute e-Alert

December 2, 2002

Dear Reader,

The new Homeland Security Act is designed to protect Americans from terrorist attacks. But you may be comforted to find out that an additional provision was added to the act so that American corporations will also be protected from the parents of autistic children.

Before the age of two, most infants in America receive 18 vaccinations, and on average about 12 of them contain a preservative that's loaded with mercury. The evidence that mercury poisoning from those vaccines sometimes causes autism in otherwise healthy kids is so overwhelming that it's got plenty of people very scared. And no one is more scared than the executives at Eli Lilly, the drug giant that makes thimerosal, the mercury-based vaccine preservative.

The higher-ups at Lilly are addressing this situation aggressively. Are they making sure that not one child will ever again be injected with a vaccine containing mercury? No. But they are going to enormous trouble and expense to protect their company from lawsuits filed against them by parents whose children now suffer severe neurological damage. And this protection comes courtesy of the U.S. Senate, through the Homeland Security Act, signed into law just a few days ago.

Two articles about this controversy appeared in the New York Times last week. The first made me angry – then the second just made me angrier. Because this transparent "gift" to a well-connected drug company gets more and more unseemly with each new revelation.

A ticking bomb

More than 75 years ago, Eli Lilly Company developed thimerosal, the vaccine preservative that contains approximately 50% mercury. In recent decades, scientists have shown that mercury is a dangerous neurotoxin. No surprise then that the high levels of mercury detected in many young children in America have been directly linked to permanent neurological damage, including autism. And the one thing all of these children have in common is that they received multiple vaccinations, beginning in the first months of their lives.

Lilly denies this connection, of course. But it obviously scares the heck out of them. Even the FDA has admitted the connection, although this admission is couched in the softest possible language, stating that "concerns" have been raised, and claiming that the agency is working with vaccine manufacturers to "reduce or eliminate thimerosal from vaccines." And even though it sounds as light as air, we know the FDA doesn't make this sort of statement lightly. Especially when a major drug company has so much at stake.

Defusing the bomb

But when you run an international pharmaceutical company, you don't just let the chips fall where they may. Not at all – you get out there and flex some influential muscle.

During the recent political season, Lilly donated $1.6 million dollars to various candidates – more than any other pharmaceutical company. So it hardly seems like a mysterious coincidence that less than two weeks after the mid-term elections someone in the senate sneaked this vaccine provision into the homeland security bill. And "sneaked" is no exaggeration – the provision was introduced at the 11th hour, as were six other provisions that had nothing whatsoever to do with homeland security. But while tucking "pork" into bills that are about to pass is business-as-usual for congress, the unusual thing about this particular pork chop is that no one is taking credit for it.

As The New York Times reported last Friday, nobody seems to know, or will admit to knowing, who placed the provision in the bill, or even who wrote it. It's almost as if someone is ashamed to be associated with this addition that will simply brush aside both class-action and individual thimerosal lawsuits aimed at Eli Lilly. A spokesman for Lilly said that the company knew absolutely nothing about the sweetheart provision.

Right.

I suppose that includes Sidney Taural, the chairman, president and C.E.O. of Eli Lilly, who has a seat on President Bush's Homeland Security Advisory Council.

Right.

"Working" it out

Well none of this has a very good smell, does it? Even the current senate minority leader Trent Lott recognizes the fishy odor. So to force through the passage of the Homeland Security bill, Senator Lott promised that three of the last-minute provisions (including the vaccine protection) would be reviewed when congress reconvenes next year. He said, "We need to work on those three provisions."

Note that he didn't say that the provisions would be removed, reworded, or changed. He only said, "we need to work" on them. And that's a perfect example of some beautifully vague political-speak for you.

Meanwhile, the provision currently stands as law, sufficiently complicating all of those existing lawsuits. It will be very interesting to see just how diligently Senator Lott's "work" proceeds on behalf of a handful of citizens against a deep-pockets pharmaceutical giant like Lilly.

Don't get me wrong. I am not a proponent of litigation. But this is not a hot cup of coffee at McDonald's we're talking about. And even if it were, the way it was swept off the table is shameful.

Take care of the kids

Last year, under pressure from the Centers for Disease Control, the Public Health Service, and the American Academy of Pediatrics, pharmaceutical companies agreed to stop manufacturing vaccines that contain thimerosal. But while this mercury-based preservative is no longer in production, stores of vaccines that contain it are still being used. This is a very important detail that all parents of young children should know about because they can tell their pediatricians to use only thimerosal-free vaccines on their children.

Courtney L. Zietzke

Whether or not you're a parent of young children, I hope you'll share this critical information with friends and loved ones whose children are young enough to receive vaccinations. Likewise, if you have a child or know of a child who is showing signs of autism, you can get further information and assistance from the Coalition for SAFE MINDs (Sensible Action For Ending Mercury-Induced Neurological Disorders) – a non-profit organization founded by parents to raise awareness about the exposure to mercury from medical products (safeminds.org).

Personally, I am going to take a few minutes to write to Senators Mikulski and Sarbanes and let them know that I don't consider autistic children terrorists from whom we require protection. You know, for when they "work" on those last-minute provisions.

News | Undergraduate | People | Online Courses | Mulimedia Events | Forms | Links | Home

The University of Minnesota is an equal opportunity educator and employer.

Read our *Privacy Statement*

Page Coordinator: *mcoleman@d.umn.edu & msulliv1@d. umn.edu.*

Last Modified on: Saturday, 21l-Dec-2002 19:41:17 CST

Exhibit # 6

Public Domain

Global Drug Industry Launches All-Out Attack on Rights of Thimerosal-Injured Children

Thimerosal is a mercury-based additive to vaccines that has potentially poisoned hundreds of thousands of American children. Faced with the prospect of thousands of lawsuits seeking compensation for the devastating injuries caused by thimerosal poisoning, the international pharmaceutical companies and t heir army of lobbyists are pushing a bill in Congress to wipe out the rights of children and their families to get legal relief. Rather than seek an answer in a fair court, these corporations have instructed Senator Frist to champion legislation that would refuse these children their day in court. Sponsored by Senator Bill Frist (Republican, TN), the legislation known as *SB 2053* or "the Frist Bill" would:

• require that every thimerosal-injury lawsuit currently pending anywhere in America be immediately dismissed

• force thimerosal injury claims into a bureaucratic administrative program in Washington, DC that is not designed to handle these claims

• prohibit any judge from ordering the drug companies to provide the money for desperately needed research and medical monitoring of children exposed to thimerosal

• forever deprive any child over the age of 8 of any legal remedy whatsoever, either in the courts or in the federal administrative program

• prohibit class action lawsuits related to thimerosal injuries and thimerosal exposure

This website will give you the *background information* and tools you need to defeat this anti-child, anti-justice, pro-industry bill. Time is of the essence, and making sure your voice as well of the voices of your friends and families need to be heard in Congress to stop this terrible bill.

Please send the following text to your Senator or the Health Committee Members listed on this page:

Senator,

I believe that every citizen of this country has the right to a fair pursuit of justice when wronged.

The drug companies are attempting to move Frist Bill SB2053 forward quickly. It is set for a hearing in front of Sen Kennedy's Health Committee.

I am asking you to refuse SB2053 (the "Frist Bill"). It is anti-child, pro-corporation and anti-justice.

The Frist Bill addresses thimerosal and is specifically putting corporate welfare before that of our children. Thimerosal is a mercury-based preservative that may have damaged thousands of children. These children and their families have the right to pursue this issue in court. The Frist Bill blocks that right unilaterally and in perpetuity in all venues.

I ask you, Senator, as a protector of our nation to choose our children over the corporations in this matter and stop the Frist Bill from going forward.

Exhibit # 7
Public Domain: Freedom of Information Act

CONFIDENTIAL DO NOT COPY OR RELEASE

Thimerosal VSD study

Phase I

Update

2/29/00

Thomas Verstraeten, Robert Davis, Frank DeStefano

CONFIDENTIAL DO NOT COPY OR RELEASE

Following is an update on the proceedings and findings so far of the first phase of this proposed two phased study. I have used the original protocol as outline for this update.

Study design:

Retrospective cohort study using the Vaccine Safety Datalink (VSD) automated data.

Eligibility criteria:

Eligibility was restricted to children who meet the following criteria:

1. Born in 1992 or later.

2. Eligible HMO member since birth (i.e. "born into the HMO").

3. Continuously enrolled until the first birthday

The following children were excluded from the analyses:

• Premature and severe premature children. Prematurity was defined as birthweight of 1000-2499 grams or gestational age of 28 – 37 completed weeks. Severe prematurity was defined as birthweight of less than 1000 g or less than 28 completed weeks. We identified these children by the ICD9 code 765.

• Children that did not receive two polio vaccines by the age of 1. This condition was set to avoid including children enrolled in the HMO that did not use the services. Polio was considered the most commonly accepted vaccination.

• Children that received hepatitis B immunoglobulin, as these were more likely to have higher exposure and outcome levels.

• Children that had the diagnosis before the age at which the exposure was assessed.

• Children in whom any major congenital or perinatal problem occurred (including any unspecified problem involving the cardiac, respiratory or central nervous system).

• Children that remained longer than 10 days in the birth hospital or were hospitalized for any period over 10 days in the first three months of life.

Case definition:

A case was defined as any child that was diagnosed with one of the neurologic or renal conditions, listed in the annex. No distinction was made on whether a diagnosis was made in the clinic or hospital setting.

Exposure assessment:

Age-related cumulative exposure levels were derived from the automated data at 1 and 3 months of age.

Confounders and Effect Modifiers:

The following variables were included in the analyses: HMO site, year and month of birth, gender.

Statistical analysis:

We used proportional hazards models for all risk analyses, stratified by site, year and month of birth and adjusted for gender.

The startpoint was the date of birth or Jan 1st 95 for children born into NCK before this date (no OPD data available).

The endpoint was defined as the first of the following dates:

• the date of first diagnosis

• the first date that a child stopped being enrolled in the HMO

• December 31st, 97

The diagnoses were analyzed grouped in categories (neurologic developmental and renal) and individually if we encountered at least 50 cases. Because of the low number of cases, the heterogeneity of disorders or lack of specificity of the ICD9 codes (unspecified, other …) we did not pursue analyses of the "degenerative neurologic" and "other neurologic" categories as a group, but only for the following diagnoses: epilepsy, acquired obstructive hydrocephalus and infantile cerebral palsy.

A separate analysis was done for premature infants with birthweight between as this group was found to have certain vaccination characteristics (total?? vaccines in the first year of life, use of Hepatitis B vaccine) similar to the?? By limiting to this group, we intended to avoid the bias by indication?? to less exposure (vaccination) in the group at higher risk of disease and thus?? protective effect of the exposure.

As some diagnoses are often made in the clinic setting, we included all four?? additional analyses of autism, sleep disorders, specific developmental and?? and epilepsy. To evaluate the influence of excluding the children with?? perinatal conditions, we also did the analyses for the category of neurologic developmental disorders and the speech delay for ALL infants.

We analyzed the cumulative exposure at 1 and 3 months of age. At each age identify a maximum number of exposure categories with large enough?? and comparable size. WE then used the lowest category as referent. At 1?? only able to identify two categories for the rare disorders or three categories?? common disorders. At three months we identified five categories for most?? seven categories for the three most common disorders.

Sample Size and Power:

The number of cases for the individual diagnoses varied from 1 to 1381. To RR of at least 2. we restricted the analyses of the individual diagnoses to?? least 50 children.

Results:

• *Number of eligible children:*

All children in VSD (cycle 6) 2,226,907

Born after December 31st 1991 701,307

Born into GHC or NCK 211,693

Continuously enrolled first year 121,441

Received more than 1 polio in first year 116,867

Courtney L. Zietzke

Not premature 111,239

Mother did not receive HepB Ig 111,047

Excluding congenital and perinatal problems 75,659

Stay in birth- or other hospital <10 days 75,540

• *Number of cases identified*: see attached table 2

This table gives for each category of conditions and the individual disorders, the total number of cases, the number of cases remaining after removing children with congenital or perinatal problems, the median age at the time of first diagnosis, the distribution over the two sites, the sex ratio, the distribution by year of birth and the percentage among the non-excluded that are premature.

• *Risk assessment:*

• At 1 month: see attached table 3

This table provides the relative risk estimates and their 95% CI for those disorders with sufficient sample size (50 cases)

• At 3 months: see attached graphs 1 to 14

These graphs illustrate the relative risks for each of the 5 or 7 categories of cumulative mercury exposure at three months of age and their 95% CIs for those disorders or categories of disorders with sufficient sample size (50 cases). Note that the &Y axis can be on a linear or logarithmic scale, depending on the magnitude of the CIs.

Premature children (> 1500g):

We were able to perform this analysis only for the entire category of neurologic developmental disorders. We did not exclude children with congenital or perinatal disorders as this would reduce the number of cases to below 50.

At 1 month of age, we found a RR of 0.89 (o.62, 1.28) and 1.42 (0.62, 3.28) for exposure of 12.5 and > 12.5 µg, respectively, with 0 µg as referent.

At three months: see graph 15

For all four HMOs:

For autism and the entire category of developmental delays, the relative risks found were slightly altered: see graphs 16 and 17. For the other disorders with significant numbers of cases in the two added HMOs (sleep disorders, speech disorders, epilepsy), the results were similar to those for NCK and GHC separately.

For ALL children in all four HMOs:

For the entire category of neurologic developmental delays none of the exposure groups had an increased risk (see graph 18).

For the specific group of speech delays, the relative risk did not differ from those found for the subgroup included in the above analyses (see graph 19).

Discussion:

We focused our analyses on the cumulative exposure levels at one and three months of age because as this age the central nervous system is still immature and more susceptible to mercury. Another reason for this focus was to minimize the difference between the dose given and the dose actually accumulated in the body. The half-life of methylmercury is estimated to be 45 days. If ethylmercury has a similar half-life, the dose given will not differ much from the dose accumulated at one and three months, given that most vaccines are given in the second and third month. In addition, the highest proportion of children in our cohort exceeded the EPA limits at one and three months of age (see study protocol). Whereas the exposure at three months of age is related to later exposure (children in high exposure groups will remain in high exposure groups at 6 or 12 months of age), this is not the case for exposure at one month of age. The main disadvantage with the 3 months categories is the small number of cases in the lowest groups, particularly the 0 exposure group, which forced us to define the referent group as the category below 37.5 μg, except for the more common disorders.

As for the exposure evaluated at 1 month of age, which is basically an evaluation of the neonatal hepatitis B dose, we have found a significant relationship to the outcome only for misery and unhappiness disorder (ICD9 code 313.1). We were not able to produce a graph for the RRs at 3 months of this condition as no or few cases occur in the two lower categories. The relative risk for this condition was significantly increased (2.04, 95%CI: 1.09-3.82) when comparing those with a cumulative exposure above 62.5 μg at three months compared to those with cumulative exposure equal to or less than 62.5 μg. There is a nearly significant increased risk for the category exceeding 12.5 μg at 1 month for attention deficit disorder. This group includes children that received 2 doses of HepB or their first dose of Hib or DTP in the first month of life. At three months, this positive relationship is no longer significant for any category.

As for the exposure evaluated at 3 months of age, we found increasing risks of **neurologic developmental disorders** with increasing cumulative exposure to thimerosal. Within the group of developmental disorders, similar, though not statistically significant increases were seen for the sub-group called **specific delays** (ICD9 code 315) and within this sub-group for the specific disorder **developmental speech disorder** (dyslalia, ICD9 code 315.39), and for **autism** (ICD9 code 299.0), **stuttering** (ICD9 code 307.0) and **attention deficit disorder** (ICD9 code 314.0). This increase, when comparing each category of exposure to the lowest exposure group was significant only for the entire category

Courtney L. Zietzke

of developmental disorders. For specific delays and speech disorder this increase occurs only above 25 μg.

As some of the above disorders are correlated (see table 1) we analyzed the RRs for each while excluding children with any of the other disorders and found similar results to the unconditional analyses.

Table 1. Number of common cases in some disorders

	2990	3070	3140	31539
2990	66	0	7	23
3070		59	2	15
3140			158	20
31539				830

For other disorders, the trend of the risk with increasing exposure to thimerosal was either decreasing (renal disorders) or unclear (somnambulism, mixed emotional disturbances and cerebral palsy). For epilepsy we found a significant drop of the risk when exceeding 25 µg, followed by an increasing trend. We plan to evaluate the role of earlier diagnosed convulsions in these children to better understand this finding.

To evaluate potential confounding by health care use (to identify potential sick children that may have been more likely to have the disorder and less likely to be vaccinated or, inversely, to identify those parents that bring their children in for minor ailments and are more likely to have their children vaccinated), we evaluated for each exposure level, the number of hospital and clinic diagnoses, the maximum length of hospital stay preceding the exposure and the length of stay in the birth hospital. We did not see any differences in the frequency distribution of any of these, suggesting that the categories are comparable in terms of pre-existing illnesses or health care seeking behavior of the parents.

We also looked at the number of vaccinations (DTP, Hib, HepB and complete vaccination schedule (3 Hib, 3 DTP and 2 Polio, with or without the Hepatitis B requirement) by the end of the first year of life. The frequency distribution of these differed for the lowest exposure category, but was similar about 25 µg at three months (except for HepB). This suggests that children in the lowest exposure categories get an incomplete vaccination schedule for reasons not related to health care seeking behavior. The difference between the higher exposure categories lies in the use of Hepatitis B vaccine, thimerosal free vaccines, combination vaccine of Hib and DTP or simp timing of the vaccinations. We plan to repeat the analyses stratified by one of?? measures of health care seeking behavior and up-to-dateness of immunizations.

As for premature children, we found no associated risk of neurologic?? outcomes to cumulative thimerosal exposure at one or three months. As we did exclude children with congenital or perinatal problems, however, this analysis?? be biased. When including all premature children, irrespective of their birthweight found a protective effect of thimerosal above the 25 µg level at three months,?? an avoidance of vaccination in the most severe group (which his also more likely the outcome). This is confirmed when comparing the levels of vaccination to?? birthweight groups.

When including the children from all HMOs, we noticed that the increased risk developmental neurologic disorders was no longer significant. The two added?? have either no outpatient data (SCK) or only since 1996 (NWK) and many of?? disorders in this category (emotional disturbances, attention deficit disorder,?? stammering) had no or very few cases in these HMOs, which may explain this?? The curve for autism, slightly differs as most added exposed cases are found in highest exposure categories. As mentioned before, for the other disorders the?? were similar to those for the analyses of the two original HMOs (NCK and??

When including the children with congenital or perinatal conditions, no?? was found for the broad categories of any or specific developmental delays.?? suggests an avoidance of immunization in infants at highest risk of developing?? conditions. For the specific diagnosis of speech delay this phenomenon did not??

In conclusion, we can state that this analysis does not rule out that receipt of?? containing vaccine in children under three months of age may be related to an?? risk of neurologic developmental disorders. Specific conditions that may?? detailed study include autism, dyslalia, misery and unhappiness disorder and?? deficit disorder. There is no indication that thimerosal exposure is linked to?? risk of degenerative or other non-developmental neurologic disorders or renal??

Limitations:

• We have limited our analyses to a list of potential outcomes based on prior knowledge of adverse conditions found in infants exposed to high doses of methylmercury. We cannot rule out other disorders potentially related to exposure to ethylmercury.

• We were able to evaluate only relatively severe conditions that come to medical attention, and not possibly more subtle effects that would require neuropsychological testing.

• The study was underpowered for some conditions, particularly the renal outcomes.

• Some misclassification errors may have occurred in the exposure assessment (some vaccinations, particularly the neonatal HepB dose may not have been reported).

• We were not able to differentiate between single dose thimerosal free Hib vaccines and multi-dose thimerosal containing Hib vaccines. The analyses were done assuming all vaccines to come from multi-dose vials. An analysis assuming all Hib vaccines to come from single dose-vials did not substantially alter the results.

• We have no information on some potential confounders, such as maternal smoking or fish consumption.

• We could not differentiate between the difference in effect from the preservative or active component in the vaccines. Exposure to thimerosal from vaccines is invariably linked to the likelihood of being vaccinated with Hepatitis B, DTP or Hib.

• We relied entirely on automated data and did not control its quality. This is assumed to be high for most data, but maybe less so for birthweight and/or gestational age.

Proposal for future study

As we do not expect to gain substantially more or different information from verification of the current findings through chart abstractions or case-control study, we propose to conduct a follow-up study of current of the neurophyschologic functioning of cohorts children randomly drawn from different exposure categories.

Table 2. Number of children identified per disorder and distribution by site, gender, year of birth and prematurity

Code	Description	Total	Not excl	Mean Age*	Site (%) C	W	Sex (%) f	m	Year of birth (%) 92	93	94	95	96	% Prem
ALL kids		116229	76509		82	18	50	50	17	21	19	19	22	2
	Neurologic degenerative disorders:													
330.x	Cerebral degenerations usually...	7	4	17	75	25	50	50	25	25	0	0	50	0
331.x	Other cerebral degenerative disease	59	14	16	64	36	43	57	14	29	29	7	21	0
333.x	Other extrapyramidal disease and	47	28	28	64	36	29	71	29	18	29	4	11	0
334.x	Spinocerebellar disease	8	3	23	67	33	33	67	33	0	33	33	0	0
335.x	Anterior horn cell disease	3	3	29	67	33	33	67	33	33	33	0	0	0
	Neurologic developmental disabilities:	2991	1743	27	52	48	35	65	22	27	24	17	8	4
299.0	Autism	109	67	40	85	15	13	87	30	39	25	6	0	7
299.8	Other childhood psychosis	39	22	44	86	14	9	91	41	32	18	9	0	0
299.9	Other unspecified psychosis	17	17	42	0	100	12	88	47	12	35	6	0	0
307.0	Stammering & stuttering	89	59	39	45	55	32	68	24	37	34	5	0	0
307.2	Tics	70	43	36	53	47	40	60	35	23	19	16	7	0
307.3	Repetitive movements	2	2	20	0	100	50	50	50	0	50	0	0	0
307.4	Sleep disorders	121	81	26	53	47	41	59	10	32	21	20	16	1
307.5	Eating disorders	85	35	21	96	4	42	58	13	36	33	11	7	0
307.6	Enuresis	10	4	53	100	0	25	75	75	25	0	0	0	0
313	Disturbance of emotions specific to	214	150	24	25	75	43	57	32	30	21	9	5	1
314.0	Attention deficit Sy	248	158	41	74	26	22	78	41	34	16	3	6	0
315	Specific delays in development	2163	1235	27	50	50	33	67	20	27	25	19	6	5
315.39	Developmental speech delay	1240	833	32	56	44	29	71	20	30	29	18	4	2
315.9	Unspecified developmental delay	841	363	21	43	57	40	60	15	20	21	23	17	9
317-319	Mental retardation	50	12	43	83	67	33	67	42	33	17	8	0	8

Code	Description	Total	Not excl	Age*	Site (%) C	W	Sex (%) f	m	Year of birth (%) 92	93	94	95	96	% Prem
	Other neurologic conditions:	687	256	23	81	19	43	57	25	23	22	9	4	4
343.x	Infantile cerebral palsy	289	61	22	77	23	41	59	21	13	30	23	11	7

Table 3. Sample size and relative risks for grouped and specific disorders, based on cumulative mercury exposure at 1 month of age

Code	Description	Cases	RR + 95% CI (Ref = 0 µg)	
			12.5 µg	> 12.5 µg
Neurologic developmental disabilities:		1743	1.08 (0.96, 1.21)	0.87 (0.60, 1.27)
299.0	Autism	67	0.96 (0.55, 1.68)	1.58 (0.48, 5.20)
307.0	Stammering & stuttering	59	0.97 (0.52, 1.79)	No cases
307.4	Sleep disorders	81	0.77 (0.45, 1.29)	1.74 (0.53, 5.73)
313	Disturbance of emotions specific to	150	1.44 (0.93, 2.23)	1.07 (0.26, 4.45)
313.1	Misery and unhappiness disorder	81	2.68 (1.29, 5.55)	No cases
313.8	Mixed emotional disturbances	53	0.74 (0.38, 1.44)	1.48 (0.35, 6.33)
314.0	Attention deficit Sy	158	0.96 (0.65, 1.41)	2.14 (0.99, 4.62)
315	Specific delays in development	1235	1.06 (0.92, 1.22)	0.76 (0.47, 1.23)
315.39	Developmental speech delay	833	1.11 (0.95, 1.31)	0.80 (0.46, 1.39)
315.9	Unspecified delays in development	298	1.00 (0.76, 1.32)	0.69 (0.25, 1.87)
Other neurologic conditions:		256		
343.x	Infantile cerebral palsy	61	0.93 (0.49, 1.76)	0.81 (0.11, 6.05)
345	Epilepsy	123	1.26 (0.84, 1.87)	0.78 (0.19, 3.21)
Renal conditions:		99	0.99 (0.64, 1.52)	0.36 (0.05, 2.65)
593.9	Unspecified disease of kidney	56	1.35 (0.76, 2.40)	No cases

* at first diagnosis, in months

	287	123	24	38	12	41	59	20	26	20	20	12	5
345	Epilepsy	21	39	76	24	48	52	48	29	19	5	0	5
346	Migraine	21	39	76	24	48	52	48	29	19	5	0	5
348.x	Other conditions of brain	19	19	53	47	37	63	21	26	16	21	0	5
349.82	Toxic encephalopathy												0
349.9	Unspecified disorders of nervous	29	31	76	24	34	66	31	17	31	14	3	
356.x	Idiopathic polyneuropathy	1	24										
357.x	Other polyneuropathies												
358.x	Toxic and other myoneural	3	17	33	67	67	33	33	67	0	0	0	0
359.x	Toxic and other myopathies	5	29	100	6	20	80	40	20	0	0	40	0
	194	99	22	84	16	48	52	23	22	19	19	15	3
Renal conditions:													
580	Acute glomerulonephritis	1	45	150	0	31	69	46	15	8	23	8	0
581	Nephrotic Sy	13	30	0	100	20	80	40	20	20	20	0	0
582	Chronic glomerulonephritis	5	26	0	10	55	45	32	26	26	10	6	0
583	Not specified as d nephropathy	31	19	96	10	55	45	32	26	26	10	6	0
584	Acute renal failure	3	31	80	20	60	40	40	20	0	0	40	0
585	Chronic renal failure	3	51	67	33	0	100	100	0	0	0	0	0
586	Unspecified renal failure	7	25	57	43	29	71	14	29	0	0	57	0
591.9	Unspecified disease of kidney	56	24	87	13	46	54	18	21	18	23	36	5

* at first diagnosis, in months

† The number not excluded by eliminating congenital and perinatal disorders

Graph 1: Relative risk + 95 % *CI* of <u>Developmental neurologic disorders</u> after different exposure levels of thimerosal at 3 months of age, NCK &GHC

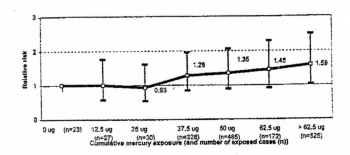

Graph 2: Relative risk + 95 % *CI* of <u>Renal disorders</u> after different exposure levels of thimerosal at 3 months of age, NCK &GHC

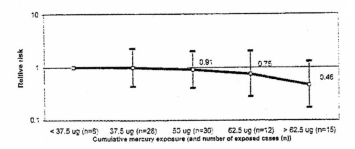

Courtney L. Zietzke

Graph 3: Relative risk + 95 % *CI* of <u>Autism</u> after different exposure levels of thimerosal at 3 months of age, NCK &GHC

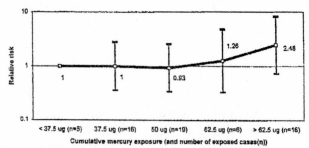

Graph 4: Relative risk + 95 % *CI* of <u>Stammering</u> after different exposure levels of thimerosal at 3 months of age, NCK &GHC

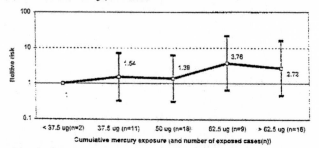

Graph 5: Relative risk + 95 % *CI* of <u>Somnambulism or night terrors</u> after different exposure levels of thimerosal at 3 months of age, NCK &GHC

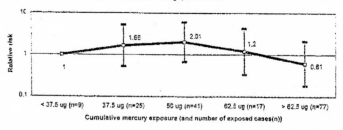

Graph 6: Relative risk + 95 % *CI* of <u>Disturbance of emotions specific to childhood</u> <u>and adolescence</u> after different exposure levels of thimerosal at 3 months of age, NCK &GHC

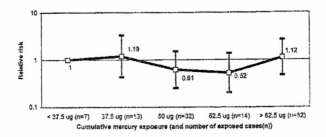

Graph 7: Relative risk + 95 % *CI* of <u>Other or mixed emotional disturbances</u> of childhood <u>and adolescence</u> after different exposure levels of thimerosal at 3 months of age, NCK &GHC

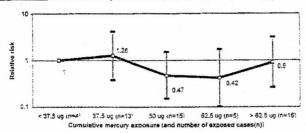

Graph 8: Relative risk + 95 % *CI* of <u>Attention Deficit Disorder</u> after different exposure levels of thimerosal at 3 months of age, NCK &GHC

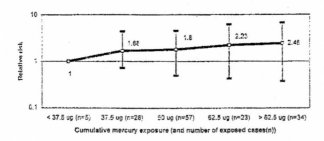

Courtney L. Zietzke

Graph 9: Relative risk + 95 % *CI* of Specific delays in development after different exposure levels of thimerosal at 3 months of age, NCK &GHC

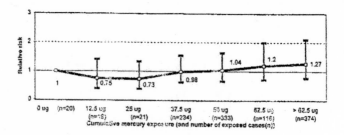

Graph 10: Relative risk + 95 % *CI* of Developmental speech disorder after different exposure levels of thimerosal at 3 months of age, NCK &GHC

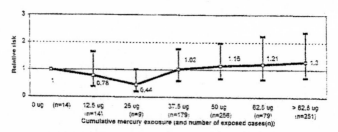

Graph 11: Relative risk + 95 % *CI* of Unspecified delay in development after different exposure levels of thimerosal at 3 months of age, NCK &GHC

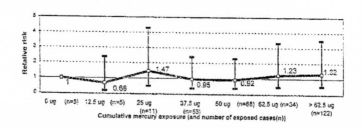

Graph 12: Relative risk + 95 % *CI* of <u>Infantile cerbral palsy</u> after different exposure levels of thimerosal at 3 months of age, NCK &GHC

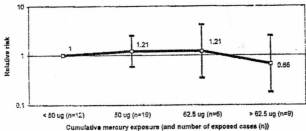

Cumulative mercury exposure (and number of exposed cases (n))

Graph 13: Relative risk + 95 % *CI* of <u>Epilepsy</u> after different exposure levels of thimerosal at 3 months of age, NCK &GHC

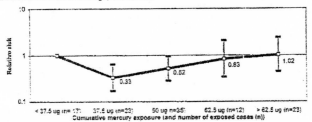

Cumulative mercury exposure (and number of exposed cases (n))

Graph 14: Relative risk + 95 % *CI* of <u>Unspecified kidney or ureter disorder</u> after different exposure levels of thimerosal at 3 months of age, NCK &GHC

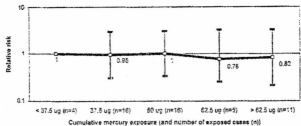

Cumulative mercury exposure (and number of exposed cases (n))

Graph 15: Relative risk ÷ 95 % *CI* of <u>Developmental neurologic disorders among prematures (>1500 g)</u> after different exposure levels of thimerosal at 3 months of age

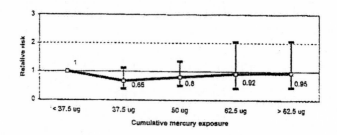

Graph 16: Relative risk ÷ 95 % *CI* of <u>Autism after different exposure levels</u> of thimerosal at 3 months of age for all HMOs

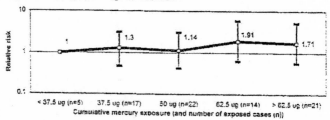

Graph 17: Relative risk ÷ 95 % *CI* of <u>Developmental neurologic disorders</u> after different exposure levels of thimerosal at 3 months of age for all HMOs

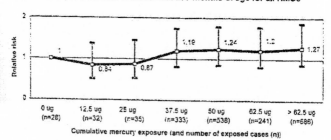

Graph 18: Relative risk + 95 % *CI* of <u>Developmental neurologic disorders after</u> different exposure levels of thimerosal at 3 months of age for ALL kids, all HMOs

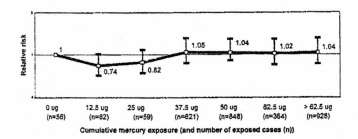

Cumulative mercury exposure (and number of exposed cases (n))

Graph 19: Relative risk + 95 % *CI* of <u>Developmental speech disorder after</u> different exposure levels of thimerosal at 3 months of age for ALL kids, all HMOs

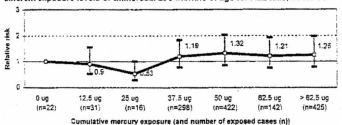

Cumulative mercury exposure (and number of exposed cases (n))

Unspecified otitis media

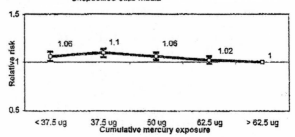

Acute URI - NOS

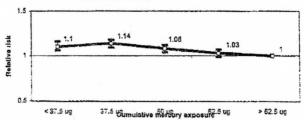

Non specific non-infectious Gastro-enteritis

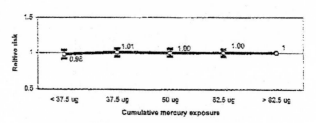

Unspecified injury

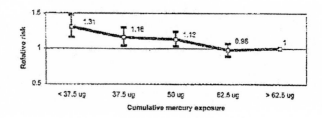

Vaccine combinations in the cumulative mercury exposure categories at three months of age:

Category	Frequency	Combinations
0 µg	2%	No vaccines
12.5 µg	2%	1 HepB only
25 µg	4%	2 HepB, 0 DTP, 0 Hib (25%)
		1 HepB – Hib, 1 DTP (25%)
		0 HepB, 1 DTP-Hib (50%)
37.5 µg	51%	1 HepB, 1 DTP-Hib
50 µg	32%	2 HepB, 1 DTP-Hib (75%)
		0 HepB, 1 DTP, 1 Hib (25%)
62.5 µg	9%	1 HepB, 1 DTP, 1 Hib
> 62.5 µg	18% (0.3% > 75 µg)	2 HepB, 1 DTP, 1 Hib

Note: DTP includes DTaP

Mercury contents (µg) HepB: 12.5, DTP(DTaP): 25, Hib: 25*, DTP-Hib: 25, HepB-Hib: 0

*: we assumed all Hib to be from multi-dose vials (thimerosal containing)

Frequency of categories of cumulative mercury exposure at three months of age, by birthyear

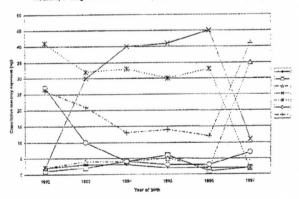

Courtney L. Zietzke

DRAFT – CONFIDENTIAL

Thimerosal VSD study- Follow-up on conference call 03/02/2000

This report summarizes additional analyses I did as a result of the many suggestions received during the mentioned conference call.

As the outcome "neurologic developmental disorders" seems to provide a reasonable summary of all important outcomes (in terms of sample size), I have restricted the following analyses to this category of outcomes.

Also for sake of reducing the number of analyses, and to keep the results easier to interpret, I have used the cumulative exposure at three months as a continuous variable. This also resolves the problem of which reference category to choose.

This follow-up report addresses the following issues:

- Ascertainment of birth dose HepB
- Socio-economic status
- Health care seeking behavior:
- Adjustment for age

- Data from NCK before 1995

The following are responses to correspondence after the conference call

- Control diagnoses
- Comparison to number of vaccines, aluminum
- Thimerosal content of Hib vaccines

1. Ascertainment of birth dose HepB

On a request by Bob Davis to give an idea on the accuracy of the birth dose for HepB in the automated data, NCK estimated the capture of the birth dose to be in the high 90% range from 7/91 onwards. GHC also expressed confidence in their capture of the birth dose from 10/92 onwards.

I tried to estimate the proportion of missed birth doses, assuming that these were missed if the automated data suggested that a child, continuously enrolled in the first two years, had had only two doses of Hepatitis B by the age of 2 years, but all the four DTP and Hib and three polio vaccinations. This approach suggested that the birth dose was not registered in 3.8% and 16.5% at NCK and GHC respectively

Alternatively, I looked at children continuously enrolled in the first year that had only 1 dose of HepB by six months, but were on schedule for DTP, Hib and Polio (at least two of each). According to this analysis, 4.2% and 17.9% of birth doses are missed at NCK and GHC respectively. Over the years there is a steady improvement at NCK from 5.9% to 3.3%, whereas at GHC, there is an improvement after an initial decline (11.8%, 22.3%, 25.9%, 15.6% and 13.6% for '92, '93, '94, '95, and '96 respectively).

These data are comparable to findings in John Mullooly's paper on data quality. Although these rates are relatively high at GHC, they probably have little effect on the thimerosal analysis as only 12.5 µg of ethylmercury to the cumulative dose is added for each HepB vaccine.

2. Socio-economic status

I linked the files to 1990 census data on blocks of homes. I then assigned race and income to the children according to which was the most prevalent in their block (e.g. if 60% was white, 30% black, 5% Asian etc, I would call the child white). Doing this I obtained the following distribution of race and income;

• Race:

White 83%

Hispanic 6.9%

Asian 6.5%

Black 3.7%

Native American 0.0%

• Yearly household Income:

Under 15 K: 6.8%

15 – 24 K: 1.1%

25 – 49 K: 66.9%

50 – 74 K: 10.8%

75 K: 14.3%

I found no association between the level of income and Hg exposure levels (at three months). Although there was a slight increase of exposure among whites and Asians (average Hg exposure at 3 months 50 µg and 49 µg vs. 46 µg and 47 µg among blacks and Hispanics) and an increased chance of the outcome among whites, stratification by race or income did not change the RR estimates.

3. HC seeking behavior: well child clinics (ICD9 codes V200, V201 and V202): these seem to be rarely recorded in both HMOs. For those approximately 10% of children in which it is recorded, there was no difference across the strata of exposure in the number of well child visits.

4. Adjustment for age (Check of proportionality assumption)

As age is equal to time in the PH model, adjusting for age is equivalent to checking the proportionality. In a stratified model one needs to check the assumption in the strata. Since the model uses over 100 strata, it would be impossible however to check this formally for every stratum. As an alternative I did subanalyses for the different years of age at which a child was right censored because of either diagnosis or stopped enrollment.

For all ages this gives: RR 1.006 (1.004, 1.010)

Under 1 year: 1.006 (0.985, 1.027)

1 – 2 years: 1.010 (1.000, 1.020)

2 – 3 years: 1.007 (0.999, 1.014)

3 – 4 years: 1.009 (0.999, 1.019)

> 4 years: 1.002 (0.990, 1.014)

There appears to be a decline in the RR after 4 years of age, but a rather constant RR before that.

As an alternative to the PH model, I also ran a logistic regression model, including gender, site, year and month of birth as covariates, exposure measure and outcome as in the PH model, imposing a minimum age of continuous enrollment for non-cases (imposing the same minimal age of diagnosis on cases removed too many of them and the model would not converge).

The RR thus obtained was

1.007 (1.002, 1.011) for no minimal time of enrollment

1.009 (1.004, 1.014) for minimal 3 years of enrollment

1.008 (1.001, 1.014) for minimal 4 years of enrollment

I conclude that the PH model does not depend on age (at least by years) and that the proportionality assumption is valid.

5. Data from NCK before 1995:

The NCK group is currently checking for a sample of the cases of speech disorder (ICD9 31539) on the date of diagnosis.

6. Control diagnoses

I looked at the relationship between the exposure and a number of frequent outcomes for which one would not expect a relationship to exist:

• Unspecified conjunctivitis

• Nonspecified, noninfectious diarrhea

• Unspecified injury

For the first two there was no trend of increased/decreased risk with increasing (thimerosal) exposure. For injury the exposure shows a significant protective effect (RR decreases .3% per μg of additional cumulative mercury exposure at three months). The relative risks for the different exposure categories are attached in Graph 1.

7. Comparison to number of vaccines, aluminum

The purpose of these analyses would be to differentiate between the effect of thimerosal and the vaccines themselves. Unfortunately (nearly) all vaccines in our analysis were either thimerosal containing (DTP, DTaP HepB and Hib) or thimerosal free (polio). Any analysis of the number of vaccines or aluminum as an exposure variable would show a correlation to the thimerosal analysis and not be helpful in the distinction. I ran analyses with the number of Hib. DTP, HepB and polio vaccines as exposure and found a relationship of the risk to the number of DTP and Hib vaccines received at three months, which was to be expected. I also found a relationship to the age at which the first Hib vaccine was given (the later the vaccine given, the less chance of neurologic developmental delay), which was also to be expected. Surprisingly, I did not find this for DTP.

To easily differentiate between the effect of thimerosal and vaccine, we would need to compare a group that received thimerosal free vaccine to thimerosal containing vaccine, which leads to point 8. The closest we have come to such a comparison was by comparing the group that received the DTP-Hib combination vaccine (containing 25 μg of mercury) to the group that received the DTP and Hib separately (each

25 µg of mercury). This comparison showed non significant relation to the outcome neurologic developmental delay.

8. Thimerosal content of Hib vaccines:

The FDA is currently matching the lot numbers to information on the exact or mean thimerosal content for all vaccines used in the two HMOs.

Graph 1. Relative risk + 95 % confidence intervals of after different exposure levels of thimerosal at 3 months of age for some additional conditions

Unspecified conjunctivitis

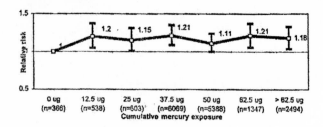

Non specific non-infectious Gastro-enteritis

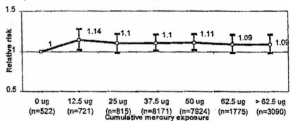

Unspecified injury

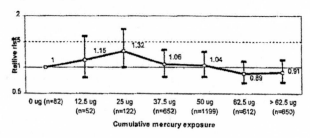

Exhibit # 8

Public Domain

From the November 2002 Idaho Observer:

FDA can't answer questions about thimerosal

There has been considerable controversy regarding the presence of thimerosal, a mercury derivative, in pharmaceutical preparations. Although the toxicity of mercury is common knowledge, the FDA has drug its bureaucratic feet over the last several years as scientists and legislators have attempted to ban its use in vaccines and other drugs. The following was transcribed from a newsclip that featured Rep. Dan Burton (R-Indiana) at a Congressional hearing Nov. 1, 2002.

[Male voice]: A U.S. Congressman tonight is calling for criminal penalties for any government agency that knew about the dangers of thimerosal in vaccines and did nothing to protect American children.

Last month a news ____ (?) investigation disclosed allegations that some government officials may have suppressed documentation about these risks.

And today some of those officials testified at a congressional hearing.

Channel 8's(?) Valerie Williams joins us now LIVE from the nation's capital with more. Valerie—-

[Valerie]: Well, obviously, the BIG concern is that thimerosal is linked to just a GROWING rate of autism among children in this country. We know from our own research that by 1972 the FDA had begun asking questions about the dangers of thimerosal. By 1992, it had been pulled out of dog vaccines and contact lens solution because of the risk, but it was not until last year that FINALLY it was removed from childhood vaccines.

Today, government health officials squirmed uncomfortably in their seats as more evidence emerged suggesting that they had mis-led the public.

[Congressman Burton]: "You mean to tell me since 1929 we've been using thimerosal and the only test that you know of is the one that was done in '29 and every one of those people had meningitis and they all died?"

[Valerie]: For nearly an hour, Burton repeatedly asked FDA and CDC officials what they knew, and when they knew it, and when memories seemed to be a bit fuzzy, the Congressman produced old memos as a refresher. This one from 1999 states that the FDA had an interim plan already in place for many years to get rid of thimerosal. The same e-mail also addresses theFDA's fear that it would (will?)

be accused by the public of being asleep at the switch for decades by allowing a dangerous compound to remain in childhood vaccines.

Burton proposes bringing criminal charges if it's proven the government agencies were involved in a cover-up.

[Female voice (Valerie?) asking Burton]: "You're (we're?) talking about a government agency –"

[Congressman Burton]: "Oh yes, I don't – look – I don't think it makes any difference whether it's a private company or a government agency; if they know they're harming somebody and they continue to let it happen then they should be held accountable."

[Valerie]: Government accountability is something that parents of autistic children have been asking for for years. Cooper Earp (sp.?) is seven. Before Cooper was three, he'd lost his ability to talk, and his mercury levels were off the charts. His parents say Cooper's only exposure to mercury was through his vaccines.

Today he has all the classic signs of autism, such as repeatedly hitting himself and fixating on things, like this spinning chair. His mother has one dream – that one day Cooper will call her "Mommy", in a sentence. "I probably have that dream once a week, that he's speaking to me and it would be wonderful."

What parents like Christy Earp (sp?) would like to ask this panel of government officials is, Why in 80 years, they have never ordered one clinical test on the effects of thimerosal in vaccines.

Congressman Burton asked the question several times today, but never got a direct answer. After the hearing, we tried –

[Female voice (Valerie?)]: "Dr. Eagan (sp?), I'm curious. Why were studies never done on thimerosal?"

[Garbled response – female voice – possibly saying "the press"]

"Dr. Eagan … Dr. Eagan. Can you please tell us why studies were never done?"

[No response]

Congressman Burton has a personal stake in this growing scandal. He says his grandsom became autistic a few days after receiving nine inoculations.

Thus far within the government, he has been a minority voice, but he has subpoena power and he keeps threatening to use it.

[Burton]: "So what you do, is you just keep making the case and you keep trying to get the message out to a broader and broader audience, so that people start saying 'Why?' And when enough people say 'Why?' then change starts to take place."

[Valerie]: Now, researchers say since the 1990s, autism rates in children have surpassed epilepsy, cerebral palsy, and mental retardation in this country. However, an FDA official today again insisted that he saw no problems with thimerosal in vaccines. Well, that's become kind of a two-edged sword because they have no studies to back that assertion up.

I'm Valerie Williams. Back to you, Missy (?) and John.

[Male voice]: Okay, Valerie, thank you.

***

The transcript above was taken from a television video clip that was found at:
www.wfaa.com/watchvideo/index.jsp?
SID=3070133

Courtney L. Zietzke

Thanks to Susan Pearce of Vaccination Liberation, Wyoming Chapter for transcribing the story above.

***

Note: On page 10 we learn that thimerosal, which was supposedly removed from vaccines last year, is in flu vaccines that will be administered to millions of Americans, babies and children included, this season.

The Idaho Observer

P.O. Box 457

Spirit Lake, Idaho 83869

Phone: 208-255-2307

Email: *observer@coldreams.com*

Web:

http://Idaho-observer.com

http://proliberty.com/observer/

Exhibit # 9

Public Document: Congressional

O:\BAI\BAI03.338 S.L.C.

108TH CONGRESS
1ST SESSION

S. _____

_____

IN THE SENATE OF THE UNITED STATES

_____introduced the following bill;
which was read twice and
referred to the Committee on _____

_____

_____

A BILL

To amend the Public Health Service Act to improve immunization rates by increasing the distribution of vaccines and improving and clarifying the vaccine injury compensation program, and for other purposes.

Be it enacted by the Senate and House of Representatives of the United States of America in Congress assembled,

SECTION 1. SHORT TITLE.

This Act may be cited as the "Improved Vaccine Affordability and Availability Act".

O:\BAI\BAI03.338 S.L.C.

TITLE I—STATE VACCINE GRANTS

SEC. 101. AVAILABILITY OF INFLUENZA VACCINE.

Section 317(j) of the Public Health Service Act (42 U.S.C. 247b(j) is amended by adding at the end the following: "(3)(A) For the purpose of carrying out activities relating to influenze vaccine under the immunization program under this subsection, there are authorized to be appropriated such sums as may be necessary for each of fiscal years 2003 and 2004. Such authorization shall be in addition to amounts available under paragraphs (1) and (2) for such purpose. "(B) The authorization of appropriations established in subparagraph (A) shall not be effective for a fiscal year unless the total amount appropriated under paragraphs (1) and (2) for the fiscal year is not less than such total for fiscal year 2000. "(C) The purposes for which amounts appropriated under subparagraph (A) are available to the Secretary inclued providing for improved State and local infrastructure for influenza immunizations under this subsection in accordance with the following: "(i) Increasing influenza immunization rates in populations considered by the Secretary to be at high risk for influenza-related complications and in their contacts. "(ii) Recommending that health care providers actively target influenza vaccine that is available in September, October, and November to individuals who are at increased risk for influenza-related com- placations and to their contacts. "(iii) Providing for the continued availability of influenza immunizations through December of such year, and for additional periods to the extent that influenza vaccine remains available. "(iv) Encouraging States, as appropriate, to develop contingency plans (including plans for public and professional educational activites) for maximizing influenza immunications for high-risk populations in the event of a delay or shortage of influenza vaccine. "(D) The Secretary shall submit to the Committee on Energy and Commerce of the House of Representa tives, and the Committee on Health, Education, Labor, and Pensions of the Senate, periodic reports describing the activities of the Secretary under this subsection regarding influlenza vaccine. The first such report shall be submitted not later than June 6, 2003, the second report shall be submitted not later than June 6, 2004, and subsequent reports shall be submitted biennially thereafter.".

SEC. 102. PROGRAM FOR INCREASING IMMUNIZATION RATES FOR ADULTS AND ADOLESCENTS; COLLECTION OF ADDITIONAL IMMUNIZATION DATA.
(a) ACTIVITIES OF CENTERS FOR DISEASE CONTROL AND PREVENTION.
—Section 317(j) of the Public Health Service Act (42 U.S.C. 247b(j)), as amended by section101, is further amended by adding at the end the following: "(4)(A) For the purpose of carrying out activities to increase immunization rates for adults and adolescents through the immunization program under this subsection, and for the purpose of carrying out subsection (k)(2), there are authorized to be appropriated

$50,000,000 for fiscal year 2003, and such sums as may be necessary for each of the fiscal years 2004 through 2006. Such author ization is in addition to amounts available under paragraphs (1), (2), and (3) for such purposes. "(B) In expending amounts appropriated under sub paragraph (A), the Secretary shall give priority to adults and adolescents who are medically underserved and are at risk for vaccine-preventable diseases, including as ap propriate populations identified through projects under subsection (k)(2)(E). "(C) The purposes for which amounts appropriated under subparagraph (A) are available include (with respect to immunizations for adults and adolescents) the payment of the costs of storing vaccines, outreach activities to inform individuals of the availability of the immunizations, and other program expenses necessary for the es tablishment or operation of immunization programs carried out or supported by States or other public entities pursuant to this subsection. "(5) The Secretary shall annually submit to Congress a report that— "(A) evaluates the extent to which the immunization system in the United States has been effective in providing for adequate immunization rates for adults and adolescents, taking into account the applicable year 2010 health objectives established by the Secretary regarding the health status of the people of the United States; and "(B) describes any issues identified by the Secretary that may affect such rates. "(6) In carrying out this subsection and paragraphs (1) and (2) of subsection (k), the Secretary shall consider recommendations regarding immunizations that are made in reports issued by the Institute of Medicine of the National Academy of Sciences.". (A) RESEARCH, DEMONSTRATIONS, AND EDUCATION.—Section 317(k) of the Public Health Service Act(42 U..S.C. 247b(k)) is amended— (1) by redesignating paragraphs (2) through(4) as paragraphs (3) through (5), respectively; (2) by inserting after paragraph (1) the fol lowing: "(2)(A) The Secretary, directly and through grants under paragraph (1), shall provide for a program of re search, demonstration projects, and education in accordance with the following: "(i) The Secretary shall coordinate with public and private entities (including nonprofit private enti ties), and develop and disseminate guidelines, toward the goal of ensuring that immunizations are rou tinely offered to adults and adolescents by public and private health care providers. "(ii) The Secretary shall cooperate with public and private entities to obtain information for the annual evaluations required in subsection (j)(5)(A). "(iii) The Secretary shall (relative to fiscal year2003) increase the extent to which the Secretary collects data on the incidence, prevalence, and circumstances of diseases and adverse events that are experienced by adults and adolescents and may be associated with immunizations, including collecting data in cooperation with commercial laboratories. "(iv) The Secretary shall ensure that the entities with which the Secretary cooperates for purposes of subparagraphs (A) through (C) include managed care organizations, community-based organizations that provide health services, and other health care providers."(v) The Secretary shall provide for projects to identify racial and ethnic minority groups and other health disparity populations for which immunization rates for adults and adolescents are below such rates for the general population, and to determine the factors underlying such disparities. "(B) AUTHORIZATION OF APPROPRIATIONS.—There are authorized to be appropriated to carry out this sub section, such sums as may be necessary for each of fiscal years 2003 through 2007.".

SEC. 103. IMMUNIZATION AWARENESS.
(a) DEVELOPMENT OF INFORMATION CONCERNING MENINGITIS.—
(1) IN GENERAL.—The Secretary of Health and Human Services (in this Act referred to as the "Secretary"), in consultation with the Director of the Centers for Disease Control and Prevention, shall develop and make available to entities described in paragraph (2) information concerning bacterial meningitis and the availability and effectiveness of vaccinations for populations targeted by the Advisory Committee on Immunization Practices (an advisory committee established by the Secretary, acting through the Director of the Centers for Disease Control and Prevention).
(2) ENTITIES.—An entity is described in this paragraph if the entity—(A) is—(i) a college or university; or (ii) any other facility with a setting similar to a dormitory that houses age-appropriate populations for whom the Advisory Committee on Immunization Practices recommends such a vaccination; and (B) is determined appropriate by the Secretary.

(b) DEVELOPMENT OF INFORMATION CONCERNING HEPATITIS.—(1) IN GENERAL.—The Secretary, in consultation with the Director of the Centers for Disease Control and Prevention, shall develop and make available to entities described in paragraph (2) information concerning hepatitis A and B and the avail ability and effectiveness of vaccinations with respect to such diseases. (2) ENTITIES.— An entity is described in this paragraph if the entity—(A) is—(i) a health care clinic that serves individuals diagnosed as being infected with HIV or as having other sexually transmitted diseases; (ii) an organization or business that counsels individuals about international travel or who arranges for such travel; (iii) a police, fire, or emergency medical services organization that responds to natural or man-made disasters or emergencies; (iv) a prison or other detention facility; (v) a college or university; or (vi) a public health authority or children's health service provider in areas of intermediate or high endemicity for hepatitis A as defined by the Centers for Disease Control and Prevention; and (B) is determined appropriate by the Secretary.

SEC. 104. SUPPLY OF VACCINES.

(a) IN GENERAL.—The Secretary of Health and Human Services, acting through the Director of the Centers for Disease Control and Prevention, shall prioritize, acquire, and maintain a supply of such prioritized vaccines sufficient to provide vaccinations throughout a 6-month period.

(b) PROCEEDS.—Any proceeds received by the Secretary of Health and Human Services from the sale of vaccines contained in the supply described in subsection (a), shall be available to the Secretary for the purpose of purchasing additional vaccines for the supply. Such proceeds shall remain available until expended.

(c) AUTHORIZATION OF APPROPRIATIONS.—There are authorized to be appropriated for the purpose of carrying out subsection (a) such sums as may be necessary for each of fiscal years 2003 through 2008.

SEC. 105. COMMUNICATION.

The Commissioner of Food and Drugs shall ensure that vaccine manufacturers receive all forms of compliance guidelines for vaccines and that such guidelines are kept up to date.

SEC. 106. FAST TRACK.

The Commissioner of Food and Drugs shall issue regulations to revise the policies of the Food and Drug Administration regarding fast-tracking and priority review approval of vaccine products currently under development, to allow for the use of new forms of existing vaccines in cases where a determination is made that applying such approvals is in the public health interest to address the unmet need of strengthening the overall vaccine supply.

SEC. 107. STUDY.

(a) IN GENERAL.—The Secretary shall contract with the Institute of Medicine of the National Academy of Sciences or another independent and competent authority, to conduct a study of the statutes, regulations, guidelines, and compliance, inspection, and enforcement practices and policies of the Department of Health and Human Services and of the Food and Drug Administration that are applicable to vaccines intended for human use that are in periodic short supply in the United States.

(b) REQUIREMENTS.—The study under subsection(a) shall include a review of the regulatory requirements, guidelines, practices, and policies—(1) for the development and licensing of vaccines and the licensing of vaccine manufacturing facilities; (2) for inspections and other activities for maintaining compliance and enforcement of the requirements applicable to such vaccines and facilities; and (3) that may have contributed to temporary or long-term shortages of vaccines.

(c) REPORT.—Not later than 6 months after the date of enactment of this Act, the Secretary shall submit to the Committee on Health, Education, Labor, and Pensions of the Senate and the Committee on Energy and Commerce

of the House of Representatives a report that contains—
(1) the results of the study under subsection(a); and (2)
recommendations for modifications to the regulatory
requirements, guidelines, practices, and Policies described
in subsection (b).

TITLE II—VACCINE INJURY
COMPENSATION PROGRAM
SEC. 201. ADMINISTRATIVE REVISION OF VACCINE
INJURY TABLE.
Section 2114 of the Public Health Service Act (42 U.S.C.
300aa-14) is amended—(1) by striking subsection (c) (1) and
inserting the following: "(1) The Secretary may promulgate
regulations to modify in accordance with paragraph (3) the
Vaccine Injury Table. In promulgating such regulations, the
Secretary shall provide for notice and for at least 60 days of
public comment."; and(2) in subsection (d), by striking "90
days" and inserting "60 days".
SEC. 202. EQUITABLE RELIEF.
Section 2111(a)(2)(A) of the Public Health Service Act (42
U.S.C. 300aa—11(a)(2)(A)) is amended by striking "No
person" and all that follows through "and—" and inserting
the following: "No person may bring or maintain a civil
action against a vaccine administrator or manufacturer in a
Federal or State court for damages arising from, or equitable
relief relating to, a vaccine-related injury or death associated
with the administration of a vaccine after October 1, 1988
and no such court may award damages or equitable relief
for any such vaccine-related injury or death, unless the
person proves past or present physical injury and a timely
petition has been filed in accordance with section 2116 for

compensation under the Program for such injury or death and—".

SEC. 203. DERIVATIVE PETITIONS FOR COMPENSATION.
(a) LIMITATIONS ON DERIVATIVE PETITIONS.—
Section 2111(a)(2) of the Public Health Service Act (42 U.S.C. 300aa-11(a)(2)) is amended—(1) in subparagraph (B), inserting "or (B)" after "subparagraph (A)"; (2) by redesignating subparagraph (B) as sub paragraph (C); and (3) by inserting after subparagraph (A) the following: "(B)(i) No parent or other third party may bring or maintain a civil action against a vaccine administrator or manufacturer in a Federal or State court for damages or equitable relief relating to a vaccine-related injury or death, including without limitation damages for loss of consortium, society, companionship, or services, loss of earnings, medical or other expenses, and emotional distress, and no court may award damages or equitable relief in such an action, unless—"(I) the person who sustained the underlying vaccine-related injury or death upon which such parent's or other third party's claim is premised has timely filed a petition for com pensation in accordance with section 2111; "(II) such parent or other third party is the legal representative or spouse of the person who sustained the underlying vaccine-related injury or death, and such legal representative or spouse has filed a timely derivative petition, in accordance with section 2116; and "(III)(aa) the United States Court of Federal Claims has issued judgment under section 2112 on the derivative petition, and such legal representative or spouse elects under section 2121(a) to file a civil action; or "(bb) such legal representative or spouse elects to withdraw such derivative petition under section

2121(b) or such petition is considered withdrawn under such section. "(ii) Any civil action brought in accordance with this subparagraph shall be subject to the standards and procedures set forth in sections 2122 and 2123, regardless of whether the action arises directly from a vaccine-related injury or death associated with the administration of a vaccine. In a case in which the person who sustained the underlying vaccine-related injury or death upon which such legal representative's or spouse's civil action is premised elects under section 2121(a) to receive the compensation awarded, such legal representative or spouse may not bring a civil action for damages or equitable relief, and no court may award damages or equitable relief, for any injury or loss of the type set forth in section 2114(a) or that might in any way overlap with or otherwise duplicate compensation of the type available under section 2115(a).".

(b) ELIGIBLE PERSONS.—Section 2111(a)(9) of the Public Health Service Act (42 U.S.C. 300aal—11(a)(9)) is amended by striking the period and inserting "and to a parent or other third party to the extent such parent or other third party seeks damages or equitable relief relating to a vaccine-related injury or death sustained by a person who is qualified to file a petition for compensation under the Program.".

(c) PETITIONERS.—Section 2111(b) of the Public Health Service Act (42 U.S.C. 300aa-11(b) is amended—(1) in paragraph (1)— (A) in subparagraph (A), by striking "(B)" and inserting "(C)"; (B) by redesignating subparagraph (B) as subparagraph (C); and (C) by inserting after subparagraph (A) the following: "(B) Except as provide din subparagraph (C), any legal representative or spouse of a person—"(i) who has sustained a vaccine-related injury or death; and "(ii) who has filed a petition for compensation under the Program (or whose legal representative has filed such a petition as author ized in subparagraph (A)); may, if such legal representative or spouse meets the requirements of subsection (d), file a derivative petition under this section."; and (2) in paragraph (2)—(A) by inserting "by or on behalf of the person who sustained the vaccine-related injury or death" after "filed"; and(B) by adding at the end the following: "A legal representative or spouse may file only 1 derivative petition with respect to each under lying petition.".

(d) DERIVATIVE PETITION CONTENTS.—Section2111 of the Public Health Service Act (42 U.S.C. 300aa-11) is amended—(1) by redesignating subsections (d) and (e) as subsections (e) and (f), respectively; and(2) by inserting after subsection (c) the following: "(d) DERIVATIVE PETITIONS.— "(1) If the legal representative or spouse of the person who sustained the vaccine-related injury or death seeks compensation under the Program, such legal representative or spouse shall file a timely derivative petition for compensation under the Program in accordance with this section. "(2) Such a derivative petition shall contain— "(A) except for records that are unavailable as described in subsection (c)(3), an affidavit, and supporting documentation, demonstrating that—"(i) the child or spouse of such person has, in accordance with section 2111, timely filed a petition for compensation for the underlying vaccine-related injury or death upon which such legal representative's or spouse's derivative petition is premised; "(ii) the derivative petition was timely filed; "(iii) such legal representative or spouse suffered a loss compensable under section 2115(b) as a result of the vaccine related injury or death sustained by such person; and "(iv) such legal representative or spouse has not previously collected an award or settlement of a civil action for damages for such loss; and "(B) records establishing such legal representative's or spouse's relationship to the person who sustained the vaccine-related injury or death.".

(e) DETERMINATION OF ELIGIBILITY FOR COM PENSATION.—Section 2113(a)(1) of the Public Health Service Act (42 U.S.C. 300aa-13(a)(1)) is amended—(1) in subparagraph (A), by striking "and" and inserting "or, as applicable, section 2111(d),"; (2) in subparagraph (B), by striking the period and inserting ", and"; and(3) by inserting before the flush matter at the end, the following: "(C) in the case of a derivative petition, that the person who sustained the underlying vaccine-related injury or death upon which the derivative petition is premised has timely filed a petition for compensation in accordance with section 2111 and that, with respect to such underlying petition, the special master or court has made the findings specified in subparagraphs (A) and (B) of this paragraph.".

(f) COMPENSATION.—Section 2115 of the Public Health Service Act (42 U.S.C. 300aa-15) is amended—(1) by redesignating subsections (b) through (j) as subsections (c) through (k), respectively; (2) by inserting after subsection (a) the following: "(b) DERIVATIVE PETITIONS.— "(1) IN GENERAL.—Compensation awarded under the Program to a legal representative or spouse who files a derivative petition under section2111 for a loss sustained as a result of a vaccine-related injury or death sustained by such petitioner's child or spouse shall only include compensation for any loss of consortium, society, companionship, or services, in an amount not to exceed the lesser of $250,000 or the total amount of compensation awarded to the person who sustained the underlying vaccine-related injury or death. "(2) MULTIPLE INDIVIDUALS.—Where more than 1 person files a derivative petition under section 2111 for losses sustained as a result of the same underlying vaccine-related injury or death, the aggregate compensation to such persons shall not exceed the lesser of $250,000, or the total amount of compensation awarded to the person who sustained the underlying vaccine-related injury or death. The special master or court shall apportion compensation among the derivative petitioners in proportion to their respective losses."; (3) in subsection (e)(2), as so redesignated by paragraph (1)— (A) by striking "(2) and (3)" and inserting"(2), (3), (4), (5), and (6)"; and(B) by inserting "and subsection (b)," after "(a),"; (4) in subsection (g), as so redesignated by paragraph (1), in paragraph (4)(B), by striking"subsection (j)" and inserting "subsection (k)"; (5) in subsection (j), as so redesignated by paragraph (1)— (A) in paragraph (1), by striking "subsection (j)" and inserting "subsection (k)"; and(B) in paragraph (2), by inserting ", or to a legal representative or spouse of a person who sustained a vaccine-related injury or death," after "death"; and(6) in subsection (k), as so redesignated by paragraph (1), by striking "subsection (f)(4)(B)" and inserting "subsection (g)(4)(B)".

SEC. 204. JURISDICTION TO DISMISS ACTIONS IMPROPERLY BROUGHT.

Section 2111(a)(3) of the Public Health Service Act(42 U.S.C. 300aa-11(a)(3)) is amended by adding at the end the following: "If any civil action which is barred under subparagraph (A) or (B) of paragraph (2) is filed or maintained in a State court, or any vaccine administrator or manufacturer is made a party to any civil action brought in State court (other than a civil action which may be brought under paragraph (2)) for damages or equitable relief for a vaccine-related injury or death associated with the administration of a vaccine after October1, 1988, the civil action may be removed at anytime before final judgment by the defendant or defendants to the United States Court of Federal Claims. Once removed, the United States Court of Federal Claims shall have jurisdiction solely for the purpose of adjudicating whether the civil action should be dismissed pursuant to this section. If the United States Court of Federal Claims determines that the civil action should not be dismissed, the court shall remand the action to the State Court. The notice required by section 1446 of title 28, United States Code, shall be filed with the United States Court of Federal Claims, and that court shall, except as otherwise provided in this section, proceed in accordance with sections 1446 through1451 of title 28, United States Code.".

SEC. 205. CLARIFICATION OF WHEN INJURY IS CAUSED BY FACTOR UNRELATED TO ADMINISTRATION OF VACCINE.

Section 2113(a)(2)(B) of the Public Health Service Act (42 U.S.C. 300aa-13(a)(2)(B)) is amended—(1) by inserting "structural lesions, genetic disorders," after "and related anoxia),"; (2) by inserting "(without regard to whether the cause of the infection, toxin, trauma, structural lesion, genetic disorder, or metabolic disturbance is known)" after "metabolic disturbances"; and (3) by striking "but" and inserting "and".

SEC. 206. INCREASE IN AWARD IN THE CASE OF A VACCINE-RELATED DEATH AND FOR PAIN AND SUF FERING.

(a) IN GENERAL.—Section 2115(a) of the Public Health Service Act (42 U.S.C. 300aa-15(a)) is amended—(1) in paragraph (2), by striking "$250,000" and inserting "$350,000"; and(2) in paragraph (4), by striking "$250,000" and inserting "$350,000". (b) DEATH AWARDS.—Section 2115(a)(2) of the Public Health Service Act (42 U.S.C. 300aa-15(a)(2) is amended by inserting "(if the deceased incurred unreimbursable expenses due to the vaccine-related injury prior to death in excess of $50,000, the award shall also include reimbursement for those unreimbursable expenses that exceed $50,000)" before the period.

SEC. 207. BASIS FOR CALCULATING PROJECTED LOST EARNINGS.

Section 2115(s)(3)(B) of the Public Health Service Act (42 U.S.C. 300aa-15(a)(3)(B) is amended by striking "loss of earnings" and all that follows and inserting the following: "loss of earnings determined on the basis of the annual estimate of the average (mean) gross weekly earnings of wage and salary workers age 18 and over (excluding the incorporated self-employed) in the private non- farm sector (which includes all industries other than agri- cultural production crops and livestock), as calculated annually by the Bureau of Labor Statistics from the quarter sample data of the Current Population Survey, or as calculated by such similar method as the Secretary may prescribe by regulation, less appropriate taxes and the average cost of a health insurance policy, as determined by the Secretary.".

SEC. 208. ALLOWING COMPENSATION FOR FAMILY COUNELING EXPENSES AND EXPENSES OF ESTABLISHING AND MAINTAINING GUARDIANSHIP

(a) FAMILY COUNSELING EXPENSES IN POST-1988 CASES>—Section 2115(a) of the Public Health Service Act(42 U.S.C. 300aa-15(a)) is amended by adding at the end the following: "(5) Actual unreimbursable expenses that have been or will be incurred for family counseling as is determined to be reasonably necessary and that re sult from the vaccine-related injury from which the petitioner seeks compensation.".

(b) EXPENSES OF ESTABLISHING AND MAINTAINING GUARDIANSHIPINPOST-1988CASES.—Section2115(a) of the Public Health Service Act (42 U.S.C. 300aa-15(a)), as amended by subsection (a), is further amended by adding at the end the following: "(6) Actual unreimbursable expenses that have been, or will be reasonably incurred to establish and maintain a guardianship or conservatorship for an individual who has suffered a vaccine-related injury, including attorney fees and other costs incurred in a proceeding to establish and maintain such guardianship or conservatorship.".

(c) CONFORMING AMENDMENT FOR CASES FROM1988 AND EARLIER.—Section 2115 of the Public Health Service Act (42 U.S.C. 300aa-15) is amended in subsection (c), as so redesignated by section 203(f)— (1) in paragraph (2), by striking "and" at the end; (2) in paragraph (3), by striking "(e)" and inserting "(f)"; (3) byredesignating paragraph (3) as paragraph (5); and (4) by inserting after paragraph (2), the following: "(3) family counseling expenses (as provided for in paragraph (5) of subsection (a)); "(4)

expenses of establishing and maintaining guardianships (as provided for in paragraph (6) of subsection (a)); and".

SEC. 209. ALLOWING PAYMENT OF INTERIM COSTS.

Section 2115 of the Public Health Service Act (42 U.S.C. 300aa-15) is amended in subsection (f), as so redesignated by section 203(f), by adding at the end the following: "(4) A special master or court may make an in terim award of costs subject to final adjustment if— "(A) the case involves a vaccine administered on or after October 1, 1988; "(B) the special master or court has determined that the petitioner is entitled to compensation under the Program; "(C) the award is limited to other costs (within the meaning of paragraph (1)(B) incurred in the proceeding; "(D) not more than 1 prior award has been made with respect to such petition; and "(E) the petitioner provides documentation verifying the expenditure of the amount for which compensation is sought.".

SEC. 210. PROCEDURE FOR PAYING ATTORNEYS' FEES.

Section 2115 of the Public Health Service Act (42 U.S.C. 300aa-15), is amended in subsection (f), as so redesignated by section 203(f) and amended by section 209, by adding at the end the following: "(5) When a special master or court awards attorney fees or costs under paragraph (1) or (4), it may order that such fees or costs be payable solely to the petitioner's attorney if—"(A) the petitioner expressly consents; or"(B) the special master of court determines, after affording to the Secretary and to all interested persons the opportunity to submit relevant information, that—"(i) the petitioner cannot be located or refuses to respond to a request by the special master or court for information, and there is no practical alternative means to ensure that the attorney will be reimbursed for such fees or costs expeditiously; Or"(ii) there are otherwise exceptional circumstances and good cause for paying such fees or costs solely to the petitioner's attorney.".

SEC. 211. EXTENSION OF STATUTE OF LIMITATIONS.

(a) GENERAL RULE.—Section 2116(a) of the Public Health Service Act (42 U.S.C. 300aa-16(a)) is amended—(1) in paragraph (2), by striking "36 months" and inserting "6 years"; and (2) in paragraph (3), by striking "48 months" and inserting "6 years".

(b) CLAIMS BASED ON REVISIONS TO TABLE.—Section 2116 of the Public Health Service Act (42 U.S.C. 300aa-16) is amended by striking subsection (b) and inserting the following: "(b) EFFECT OF REVISED TABLE.—If at any time the Vaccine Injury Table is revised and the effect of such revision is to make an individual eligible for compensation under the program, where, before such revision, such individual was not eligible for compensation under the program, or to significantly increase the likelihood that an individual will be able to obtain compensation under the program, such person may, and shall before filing a civil action for equitable relief or monetary damages, notwithstanding section 2111(b)(2), file a petition for such compensation if—"(1) the vaccine-related death or injury with respect to which the petition is filed occurred not more than 10 years before the effective date of the revision of the table; and"(2) either—"(A) the petition satisfies the conditions described in subsection (a); or"(B) the date of the occurrence of the first symptom or manifestation of onset of the injury occurred more than 4 years before the petition is filed, and the petition is filed not more than2 years after the effective date of the revision of the table.".

(c) DERIVATIVE PETITIONS.—Section 2116 of the Public Health Service Act (42 U.S.C. 300aa-16) is amended by adding at the end the following: "(d) DERIVATIVE PETITIONS.—No derivative petition may be filed for compensation under the Program later than the earlier of— "(1) the last day on which the petition for compensation for the underlying claim of the person who sustained the vaccine-related injury or death upon which the derivative petition is premised may be timely filed; or"(2) 60 days after the date on which the special master has issued a decision pursuant to section2112(d)(3) on the underlying claim of the person who sustained the vaccine-related injury or death upon which the derivative petition is premised.".

(d) TIMELY RESOLUTIONS OF CLAIMS.— (1) SPECIAL MASTER DECISION.—Section2112(d)(3)(A) of the Public Health Service Act (42 U.S.C. 300aa-12(d)(3)(A)) is amended by adding at the end the following: "For purposes of this subparagraph, the petition shall be deemed to be filed on the date on which the special master issues a cer tificate of completeness, indicating that all petition contents and supporting documents required under section 211(c) and, when applicable, section211(d) and the Vaccine Rules of the United States Court of Federal Claims, such as an affidavit and tents and supporting documents required under sec tion 211© and, when applicable, section 2111(d) and the Vaccine Rules of the United States Court of Federal Claims, such as an affidavit and supporting documentation, have been served on the Secretary and filed with the clerk of the United States Court of Federal Claims.".

SEC. 212. ADVISORY COMMISSION ON CHILDHOOD VACCINES.

(a) SELECTION OF PERSONS INJURED BY VACCINES AS PUBLIC MEMBERS.—Section2119(a)(1)(B) of the Public Health Service Act (42 U.S.C. 300aa-19(a)(1)(B)) is amended by striking "of whom" and all that follows and inserting the following: "of whom 1 shall be the legal representative of a child who has suffered a vaccine-related injury or death, and at least 1 other shall be either the legal representative of a child who has suffered a vaccine-related injury or death or an individual who as per sonally suffered a vaccine-related injury.".

(b) MANDATORY MEETING SCHEDULE ELIMINATED.—Section 2119(c) of the Public Health Service Act (42 U.S.C. 300aa-19(c)) is amended by striking "not less often than four times per year and".

SEC. 213. CLARIFICATION OF STANDARDS OF RESPONSIBILITY.

(a) GENERAL RULE.—Section 2122(a) of the Public Health Service Act (42 U.S.C. 300aa-22(a)) is amended by striking "and (e) State law shall apply to a civil action brought for damages" and inserting "(d), and (f) State law shall apply to a civil action brought for damages or equitable relief"; and

(b) UNAVOIDABLE ADVERSE SIDE EFFECTS.— Section 2122(b)(1) of the Public Health Service Act (42 U.S.C. 300aa-22(b)(1)) is amended by inserting"or equitable relief" after "for damages".

(c) DIRECT WARNINGS.—Section 2122(c) of the Pub lic Health Service Act (42 U.S.C. 300aa-22(c)) is amend ed by inserting "or equitable relief" after "for damages".

(d) CONSTRUCTION.—Section 2122(d) of the Public Health Service Act (42 U.S.C. 300aa-22(d)) is amended— (1) by inserting "or equitable relief" after "for damages"; and(2) by inserting "or relief" after "which damages".

(e) PAST OR PRESENT PHYSICAL INJURY.—Section 2122 of the Public Health Service Act (42 U.S.C. 300aa 22) is amended—(1) by redesignating subsections (d) and (e) as subsections (e) and (f), respectively; and(2) by inserting after subsection (c) the following: "(d) PAST OR PRESENT PHYSICAL INJURY.—No vaccine manufacturer or vaccine administrator shall be liable in a civil action brought after October1, 1988, for equi table or monetary relief absent proof of past or present physical injury from the administration of a vaccine, nor shall any vaccine manufacturer or vaccine administrator be liable in any such civil action for claims of medical monitoring, or increased risk of harm.".

SEC. 214. CLARIFICATION OF DEFINITION OF MANUFACTURER.

Section 2133(3) of the Public Health Service Act (42 U.S.C. 300aa-33(3)) is amended—(1) in the first sentence, by striking "under its label any vaccine set forth in the Vaccine Injury Table" and inserting "any vaccine set forth in the Vaccine Injury table, including any component or ingradient of any such vaccine"; and(2) in the second sentence, by inserting "including any component or ingredient of any such vaccine" before the period.

SEC. 215. CLARIFICATION OF DEFINITION OF VACCINE-RELATED INJURY OR DEATH.

Section 2133(5) of the Public Health Service Act (42 U..S.C. 300aa-33(5)) is amended by adding at the end the following: "For purposes of the preceding sentence, an adulterant or contaminant shall not include any component or ingredient listed in a vaccine's product license application or product label.".

SEC. 216. CLARIFICATION OF DEFINITION OF VACCINE AND DEFINITION OF PHYSICAL INJURY.

Section 2133 of the Public Health Service Act (42 U..S.C. 300aa-33) is amended by adding at the end the following: "(7) The term 'vaccine' means any preparation or suspension, including a preparation or suspension containing an attenuated or inactive microorganism or subunit thereof or toxin, developed or administered to produce or enhance the body's immune response to a disease or diseases and includes all components and ingredients listed in the vaccine's product license application and product label. "(8) The term 'physical injury' means a manifest physical illness, condition, or death, including a neurological disease or disorder.".

SEC. 217. AMENDMENTS TO VACCINE INJURY COMPENSATION TRUST FUND.

(a) EXPANSION OF COMPENSATED LOSS.—Section 9510 (c)(1)(A) of the Internal Revenue Code of 1986 is amended by inserting ", or related loss," after "death".

(b) INCREASE IN LIMIT ON ADMINISTRATIVE EXPENSES.—Subparagraph (B) of section 9510(c)(1) of the Internal Revenue Code of 1986 is amended—(1) by striking "(but not in excess of the base amount of $9,500,000 for any fiscal year)"; and(2) by striking the period and inserting ", provided that such administrative costs shall not exceed the greater of—"(i) the base amount of $9,500,000 for any fiscal year, "(ii) 125 percent of the base amount for any fiscal year in which the total number of claims pending under such subtitle exceeds 150 percent of the average number of claims pending in the preceding 5 years, "(iii) 175 percent of the base amount for any fiscal year in which the total number of claims pending under such subtitle exceeds 200 percent of the average number of claims pending in the preceding 5 years, "(iv) 225 percent of the base amount for any fiscal year in which the total num ber of claims pending under such subtitle exceeds 250 percent of the average number of claims pending in the preceding 5 years, Or"(v) 275 percent of the base amount for any fiscal year in which the total number of claims pending under such subtitle exceeds 300 percent of the average number of claims pending in the preceding 5 years.".

(c) CONFORMING AMENDMENT.—Section 9510(c)(1)(A) of the Internal Revenue Code of 1986 is amended by striking "October 18, 2000" and inserting "the date of enactment of the Improved Vaccine Affordability and Availability Act".

SEC. 218 ONGOING REVIEW OF CHILDHOOD VACCINE DATA

Part C of title XXI of the Public Health Service Act(42 U.S.C. 300a-25 et seq.) is amended by adding at the end the following: "SEC. 2129A. ONGOING REVIEW OF CHILDHOOD VACCINE DATA "(a) IN GENERAL.—Not later than 6 months after the date of enactment of this section, the Secretary shall enter into a contract with the Institute of Medicine of the National Academy of Science under which the Institute shall conduct an ongoing, comprehensive review of new scientific data on childhood vaccines (according to priorities agreed upon from time to time by the Secretary and the Institute of Medicine). "(b) REPORTS.—Not later than 3 years after the date on which the contract is entered into under subsection (a), the Institute of Medicine shall submit to the Secretary a report on the findings of the studies conducted under such contract, including findings as to any adverse events associated with childhood vaccines, including conclusions concerning causation of adverse events by such vaccines, and other appropriate recommendations, based on such findings and conclusions. "(c) FAILURE TO ENTER INTO CONTRACT.—If the Secretary and the Institute of Medicine are unable to enter into the contract described in subsection (a), the Secretary shall enter into a contract with another qualified nongovernmental scientific organization for the purposes described in subsections (a) and (b). "(d) AUTHORIZATION OF APPROPRIATIONS.—To carry out this section, there are authorized to be appropriated such sums as may be necessary for each of fiscal years 2003, 2004, 2005 and 2006.".

SEC. 219. PENDING ACTIONS.

The amendments made by this Act shall to all actions or proceedings pending on or after the date of enactment of this Act, unless a court of competent jurisdiction has entered judgment (regardless of whether the time for appeal has expired) in such action or proceeding disposing of the entire action or proceeding.

SEC. 220. REPORT.

Not later than 1 year after the date of enactment of this Act, and annually thereafter, theAdvisory Commission on Childhood Vaccines shall report to the Secretary regarding the status of the Vaccine Injury Compensation Trust Fund, and shall make recommendations to the Secretary regarding the allocation of funds from the Vaccine Injury Compensation Trust Fund.

ABOUT THE AUTHOR

Mr Courtney Zietzke is a 42 year old financial accountant from Seattle, WA. Over the last three years Mr. Zietzke has done extensive research into the causes of what many call "Autism." His opinions in this book are substantiated with proven facts and direct uncontested evidence. Mr. Zietzke like thousands of concerned parents wanted answers into what went wrong and most importantly why did this national tragedy have to happen.

Printed in the United States
26389LVS00001B/181-186